"I will never
Forget you"

To Simona Kaiyte

From Ahmed Salem

Alicat

Alicat Trading Pty Ltd
140 Albert Road
South Melbourne VIC 3205
Australia
Email: publishing@alicat.com.au

Publisher Ali Horgan
Design Canary Graphic Design
Production Angie McKenzie

First published 2010

Printed in China 5 4 3 2 1

INSPIRATIONAL QUOTATIONS

WISDOM of LOVE

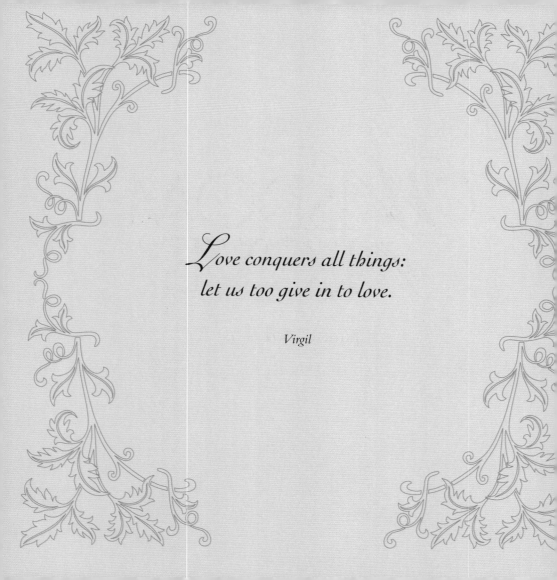

Love conquers all things:
let us too give in to love.

Virgil

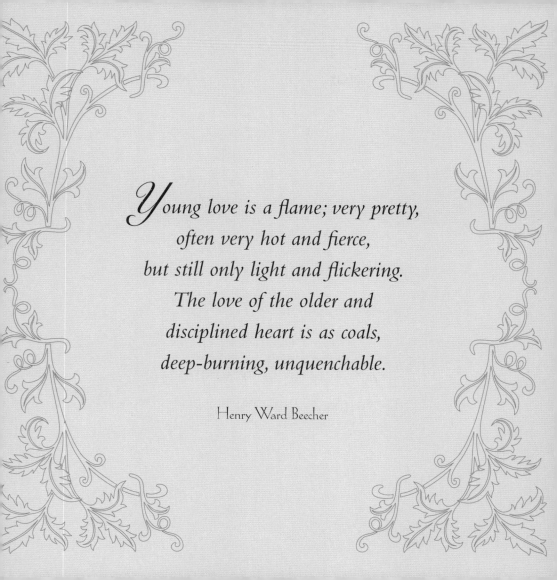

*Young love is a flame; very pretty,
often very hot and fierce,
but still only light and flickering.
The love of the older and
disciplined heart is as coals,
deep-burning, unquenchable.*

Henry Ward Beecher

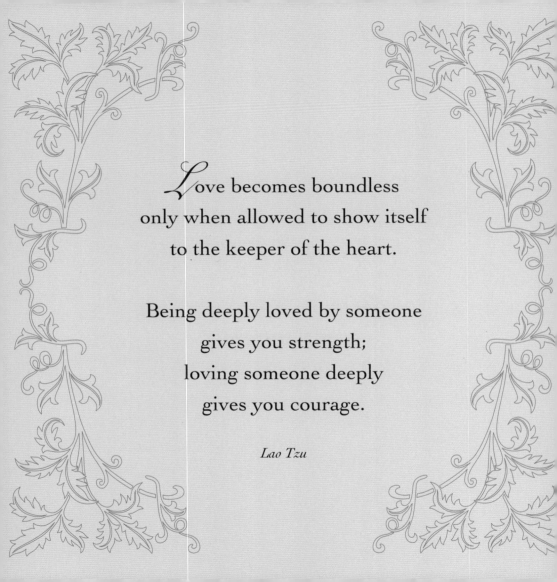

$\mathcal{L}$ove becomes boundless
only when allowed to show itself
to the keeper of the heart.

Being deeply loved by someone
gives you strength;
loving someone deeply
gives you courage.

Lao Tzu

$\mathcal{A}$ Lover's Gift

It is charming upon his gentle lips,
with those sweet eyes,
as the tenderness of his
words take flight
with the kindness that he brings.
This is my lover's gift.

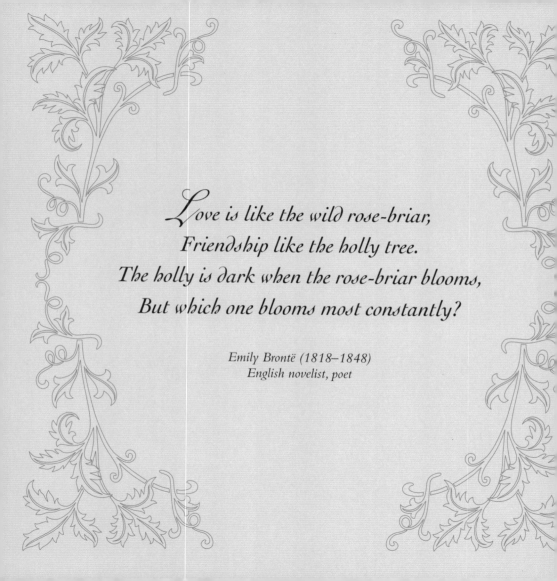

Love is like the wild rose-briar,
Friendship like the holly tree.
The holly is dark when the rose-briar blooms,
But which one blooms most constantly?

Emily Brontë (1818–1848)
English novelist, poet

Everlasting love awakens the soul.

$\mathcal{F}$ulfill ye my joy,
that ye be likeminded,
having the same love,
being of one accord,
of one mind.

PHILIPPIANS 2: 2

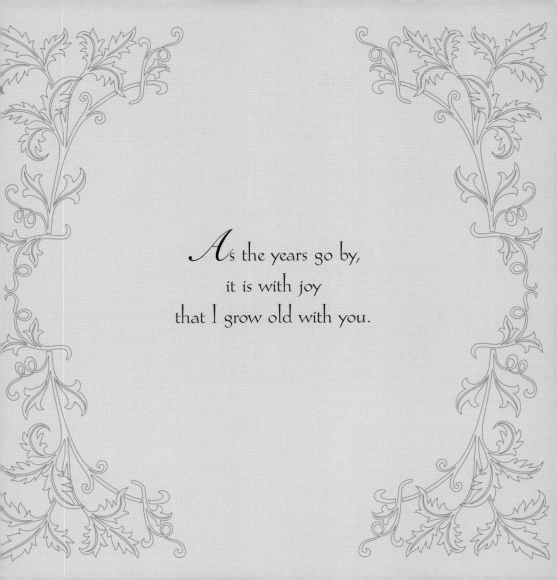

As the years go by,
it is with joy
that I grow old with you.

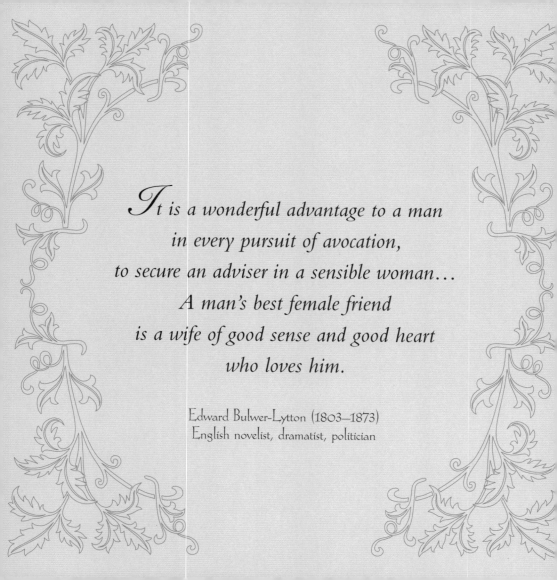

*It is a wonderful advantage to a man
in every pursuit of avocation,
to secure an adviser in a sensible woman…
A man's best female friend
is a wife of good sense and good heart
who loves him.*

Edward Bulwer-Lytton (1803–1873)
English novelist, dramatist, politician

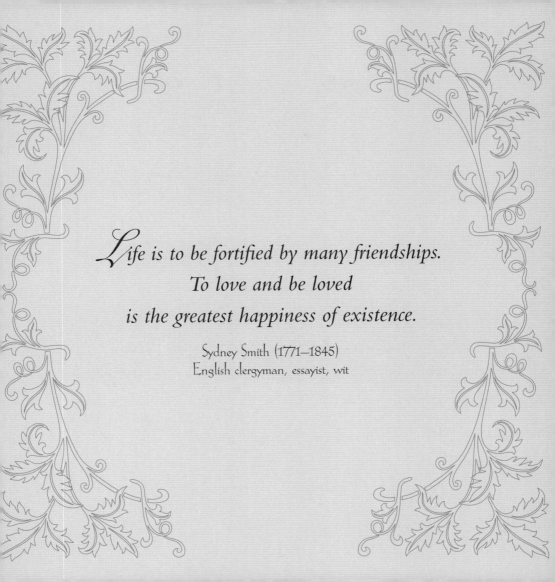

Life is to be fortified by many friendships.
To love and be loved
is the greatest happiness of existence.

Sydney Smith (1771–1845)
English clergyman, essayist, wit

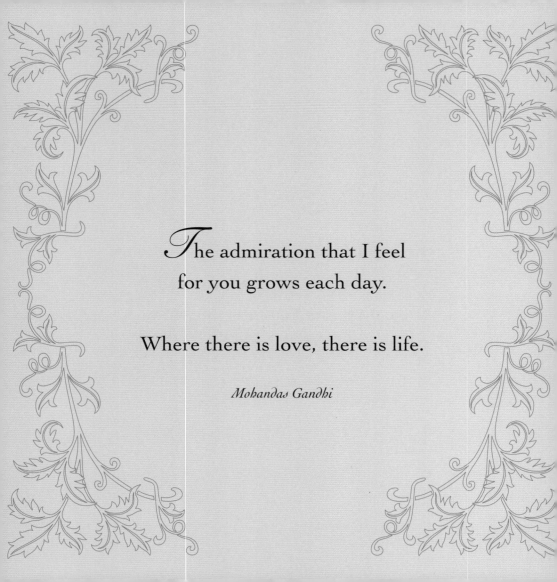

*T*he admiration that I feel
for you grows each day.

Where there is love, there is life.

Mohandas Gandhi

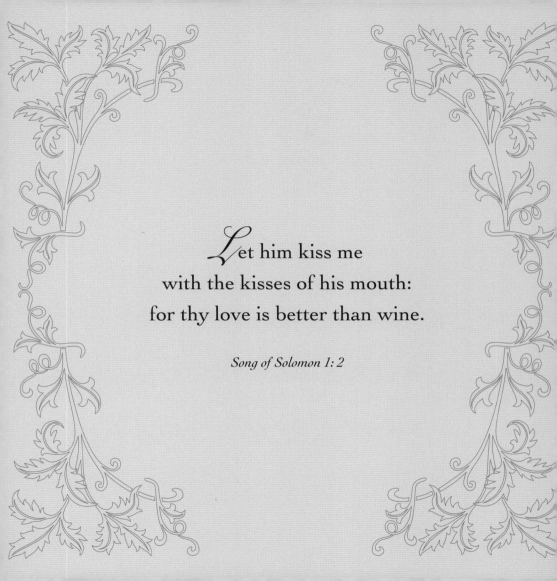

*L*et him kiss me
with the kisses of his mouth:
for thy love is better than wine.

Song of Solomon 1: 2

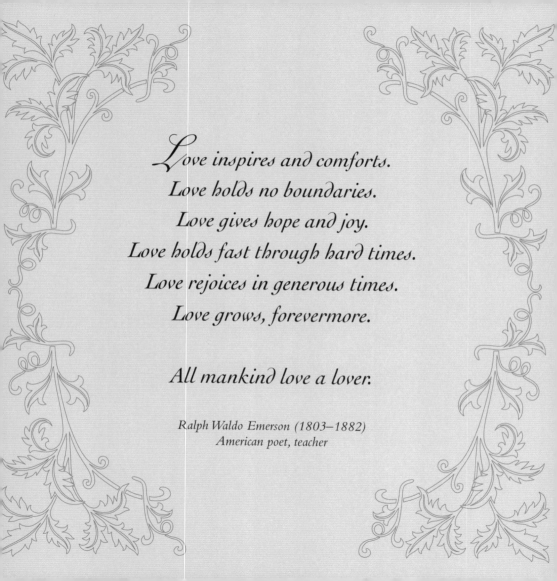

Love inspires and comforts.
Love holds no boundaries.
Love gives hope and joy.
Love holds fast through hard times.
Love rejoices in generous times.
Love grows, forevermore.

All mankind love a lover.

Ralph Waldo Emerson (1803–1882)
American poet, teacher

And walk in love,
as Christ also hath loved us.

Ephesians 5: 2

The important thing was to love
rather than to be loved.

W. SOMERSET MAUGHAM (1874–1965)
ENGLISH WRITER, DRAMATIST, PHYSICIAN

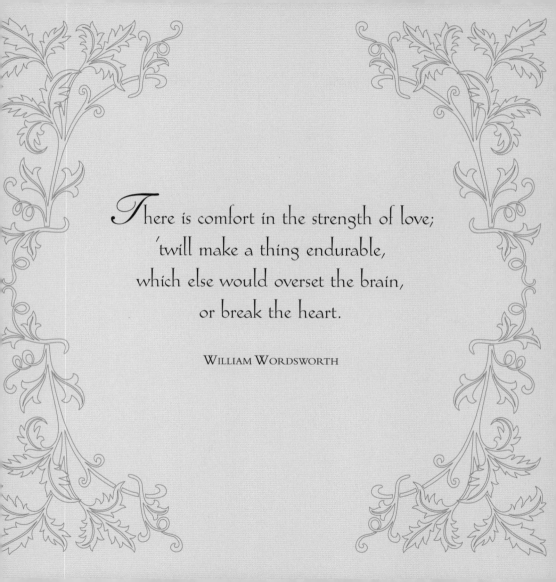

*T*here is comfort in the strength of love;
'twill make a thing endurable,
which else would overset the brain,
or break the heart.

WILLIAM WORDSWORTH

*Love shows its lover the breath of life
that comes from a single touch.*

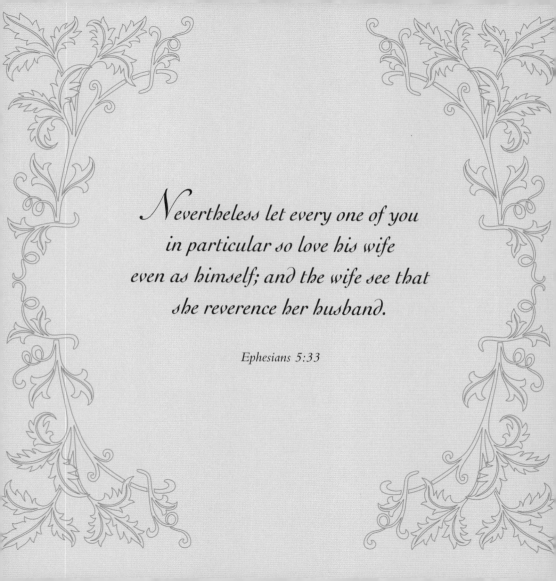

$\mathcal{N}$evertheless let every one of you
in particular so love his wife
even as himself; and the wife see that
she reverence her husband.

Ephesians 5:33

*W*ho, being loved, is poor?

OSCAR WILDE (1854–1900)
IRISH DRAMATIST, NOVELIST, WIT

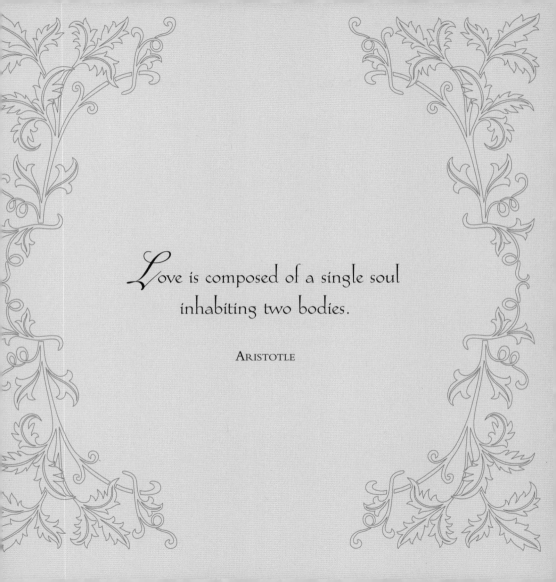

*L*ove is composed of a single soul
inhabiting two bodies.

ARISTOTLE

You will find as you look
back upon your life
that the moments when you
have truly lived
are the moments when you
have done things
in the spirit of love.

Henry Drummond (1853–1897)
Scottish evangelical writer

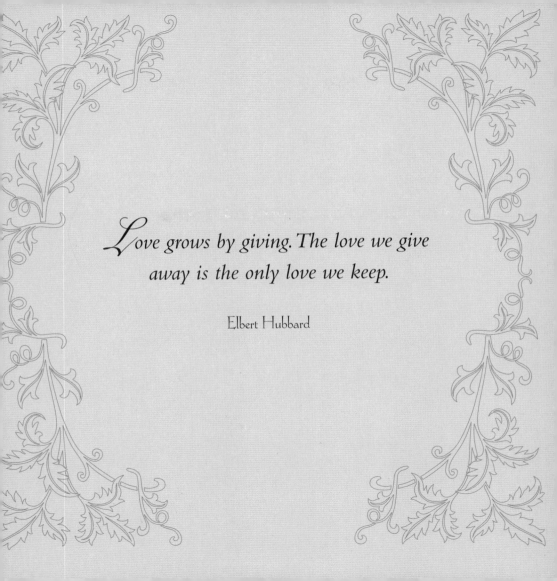

*Love grows by giving. The love we give
away is the only love we keep.*

Elbert Hubbard

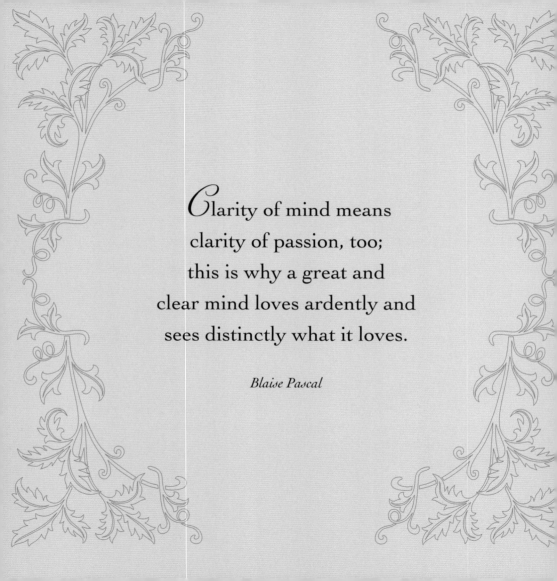

Clarity of mind means
clarity of passion, too;
this is why a great and
clear mind loves ardently and
sees distinctly what it loves.

Blaise Pascal

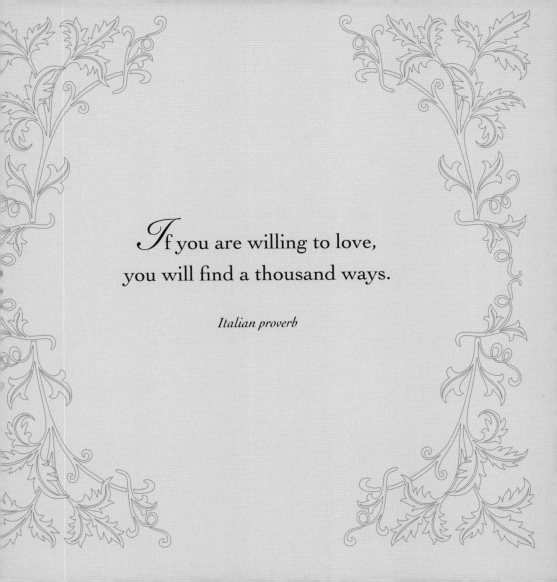

*I*f you are willing to love,
you will find a thousand ways.

Italian proverb

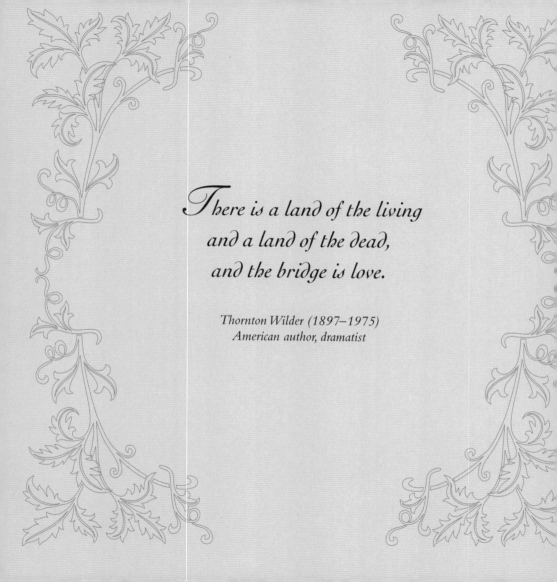

$\mathcal{T}$here is a land of the living
and a land of the dead,
and the bridge is love.

Thornton Wilder (1897–1975)
American author, dramatist

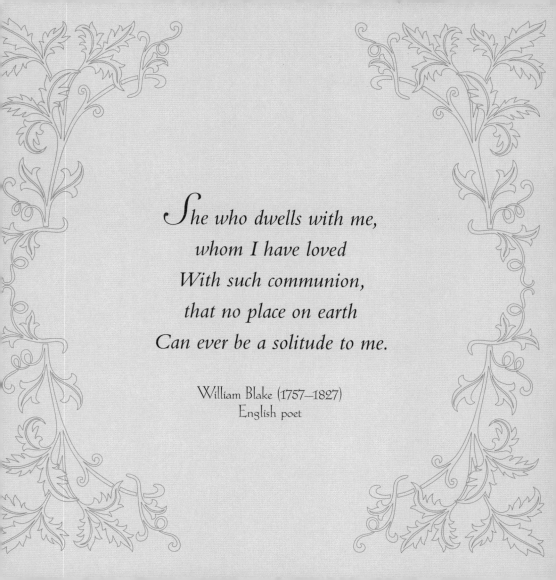

She who dwells with me,
whom I have loved
With such communion,
that no place on earth
Can ever be a solitude to me.

William Blake (1757–1827)
English poet

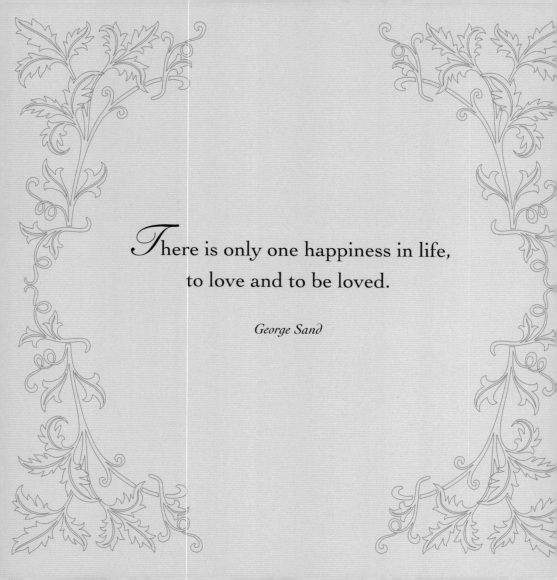

There is only one happiness in life,
to love and to be loved.

George Sand

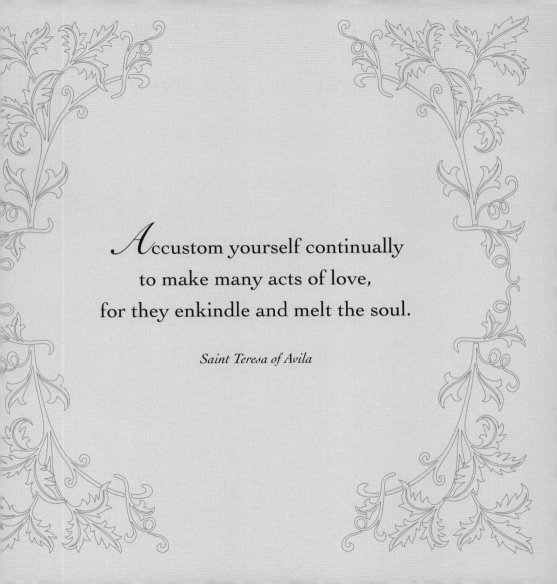

*A*ccustom yourself continually
to make many acts of love,
for they enkindle and melt the soul.

Saint Teresa of Avila

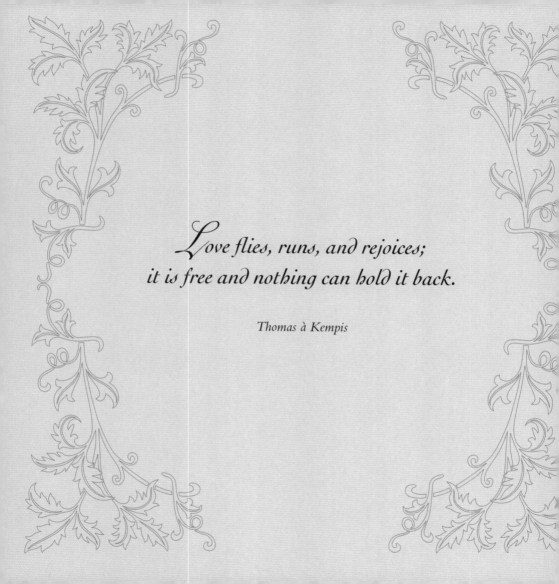

*Love flies, runs, and rejoices;
it is free and nothing can hold it back.*

Thomas à Kempis

Gravitation is not responsible for people falling in love.

Albert Einstein (1879–1955)
German–born American physicist

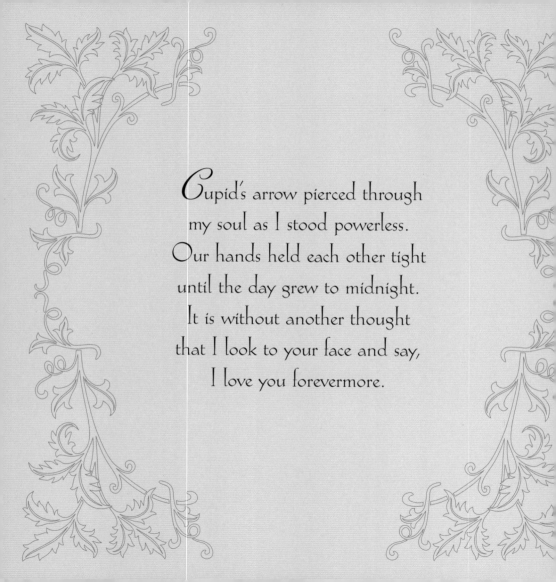

Cupid's arrow pierced through
my soul as I stood powerless.
Our hands held each other tight
until the day grew to midnight.
It is without another thought
that I look to your face and say,
I love you forevermore.

At the touch of love, everyone
becomes a poet.

PLATO (427–347 BC)
GREEK PHILOSOPHER

*One word frees us of all weight
and pain of life: that word is love.*

Sophocles

Womanliness means only motherhood;
All love begins and ends there.

Robert Browning (1812–1889)
English poet

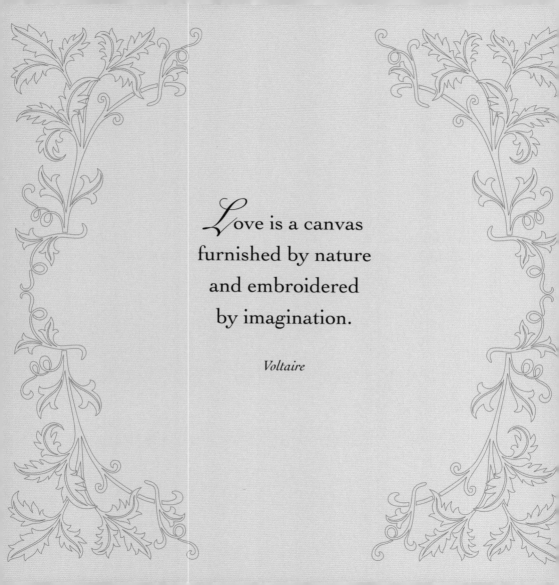

*L*ove is a canvas
furnished by nature
and embroidered
by imagination.

Voltaire

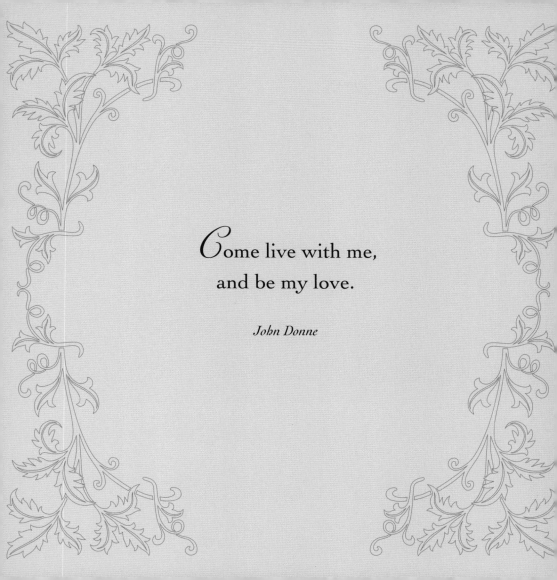

$\mathcal{C}$ome live with me,
and be my love.

John Donne

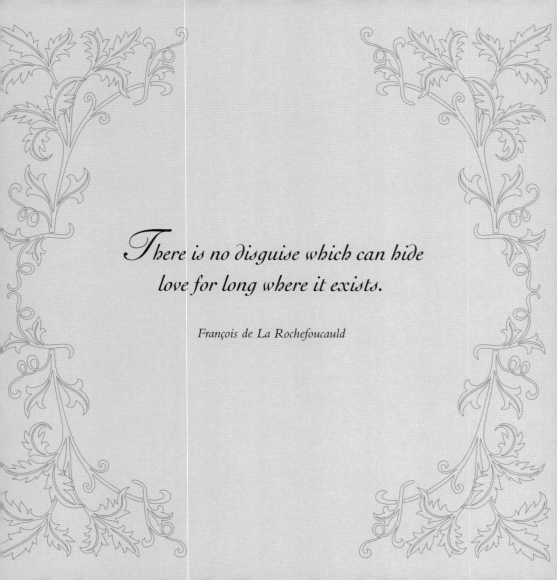

*There is no disguise which can hide
love for long where it exists.*

François de La Rochefoucauld

Love endures the test of time and overshadows it into eternity.

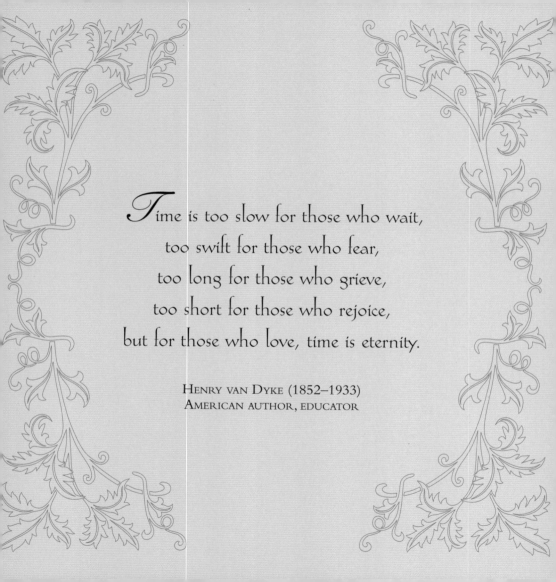

Time is too slow for those who wait,
too swift for those who fear,
too long for those who grieve,
too short for those who rejoice,
but for those who love, time is eternity.

HENRY VAN DYKE (1852–1933)
AMERICAN AUTHOR, EDUCATOR

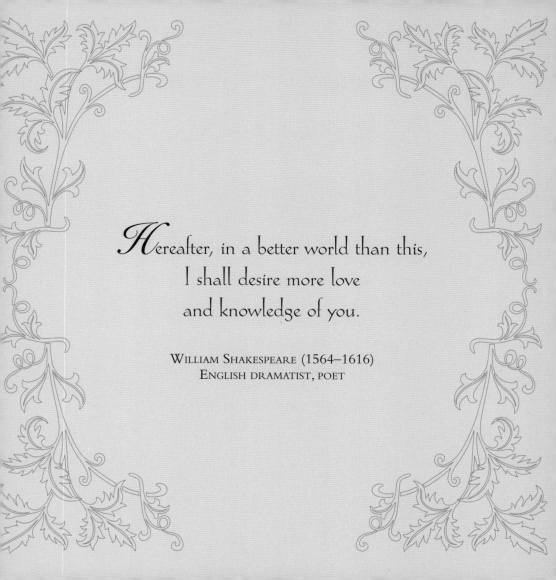

*H*ereafter, in a better world than this,
I shall desire more love
and knowledge of you.

WILLIAM SHAKESPEARE (1564–1616)
ENGLISH DRAMATIST, POET

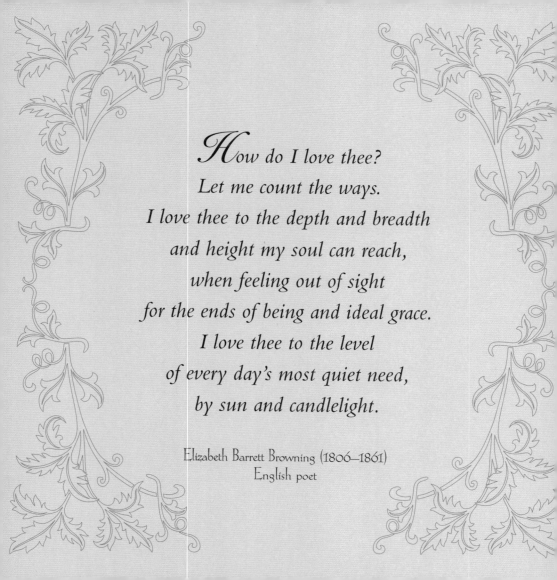

How do I love thee?
Let me count the ways.
I love thee to the depth and breadth
and height my soul can reach,
when feeling out of sight
for the ends of being and ideal grace.
I love thee to the level
of every day's most quiet need,
by sun and candlelight.

Elizabeth Barrett Browning (1806–1861)
English poet

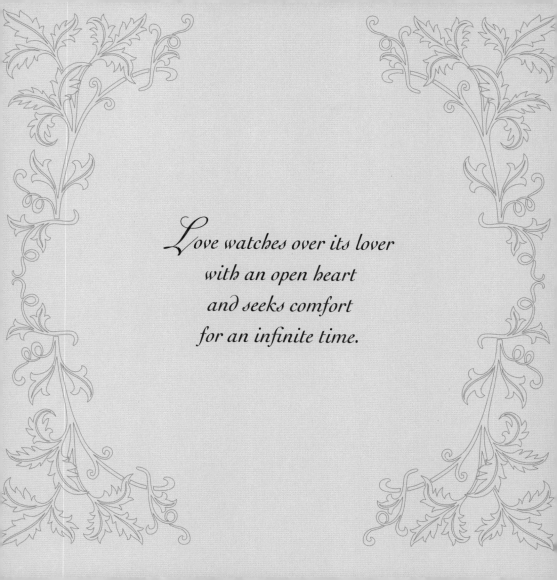

Love watches over its lover
with an open heart
and seeks comfort
for an infinite time.

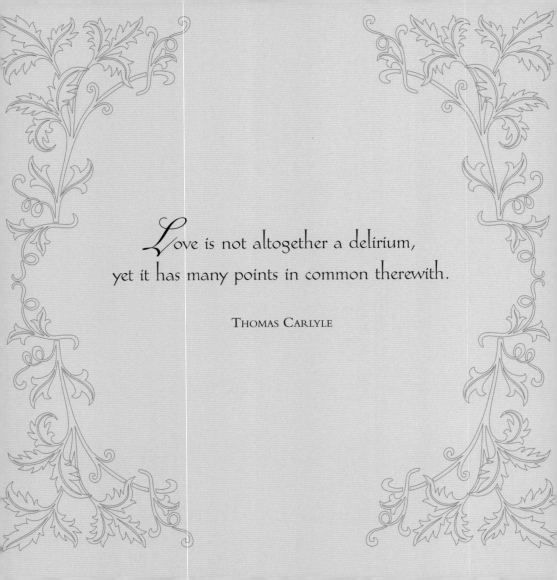

*L*ove is not altogether a delirium,
yet it has many points in common therewith.

THOMAS CARLYLE

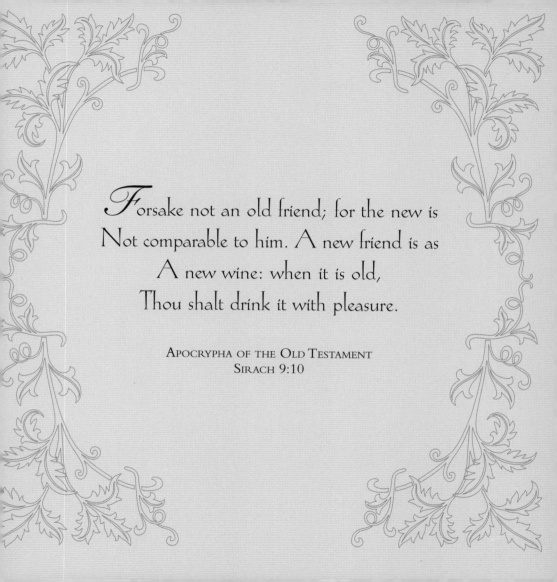

𝓕orsake not an old friend; for the new is
Not comparable to him. A new friend is as
A new wine: when it is old,
Thou shalt drink it with pleasure.

APOCRYPHA OF THE OLD TESTAMENT
SIRACH 9:10

The sweetest joy,
the wildest woe
is love.

Pearl Bailey

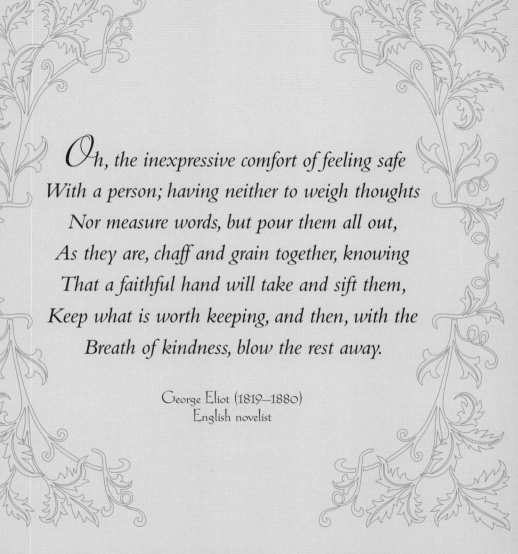

Oh, the inexpressive comfort of feeling safe
With a person; having neither to weigh thoughts
Nor measure words, but pour them all out,
As they are, chaff and grain together, knowing
That a faithful hand will take and sift them,
Keep what is worth keeping, and then, with the
Breath of kindness, blow the rest away.

George Eliot (1819–1880)
English novelist

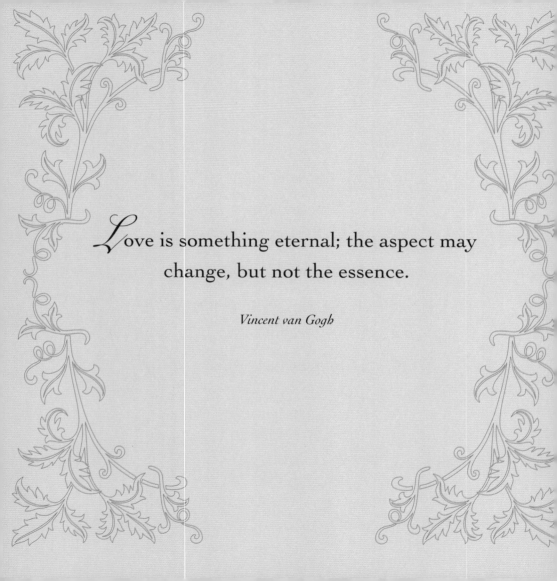

*L*ove is something eternal; the aspect may change, but not the essence.

Vincent van Gogh

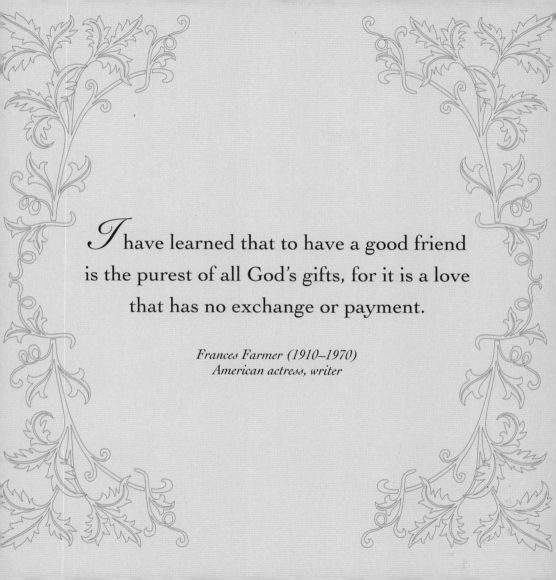

$\mathscr{I}$ have learned that to have a good friend
is the purest of all God's gifts, for it is a love
that has no exchange or payment.

Frances Farmer (1910–1970)
American actress, writer

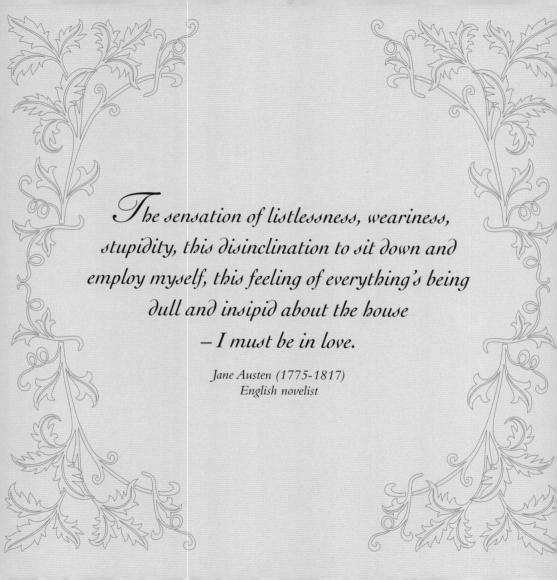

The sensation of listlessness, weariness, stupidity, this disinclination to sit down and employ myself, this feeling of everything's being dull and insipid about the house
— I must be in love.

Jane Austen (1775-1817)
English novelist

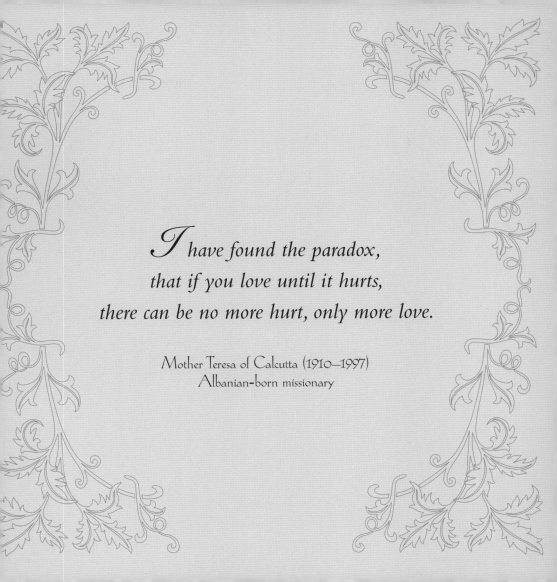

*I have found the paradox,
that if you love until it hurts,
there can be no more hurt, only more love.*

Mother Teresa of Calcutta (1910–1997)
Albanian-born missionary

$\mathcal{M}$y love is not common love,

it may be a sin to love. I say it might have

been a sin when I was another's but I had then

more merit in trying to suppress it.

I am not Free and I must sin on and love Him

more than ever, it is a crime worth going

to Hell for. For should I not be an ungrateful

unfeeling wretch not to pay two-fold with love

the man that so idolises me, that adores me.

May God only spare Him and send Him safe back.

I shall be at Merton till I see Him

as He particularly wishes our first meeting

should be there...

Emma, Lady Hamilton (circa 1761–1815)
Writing of her love for Lord Nelson

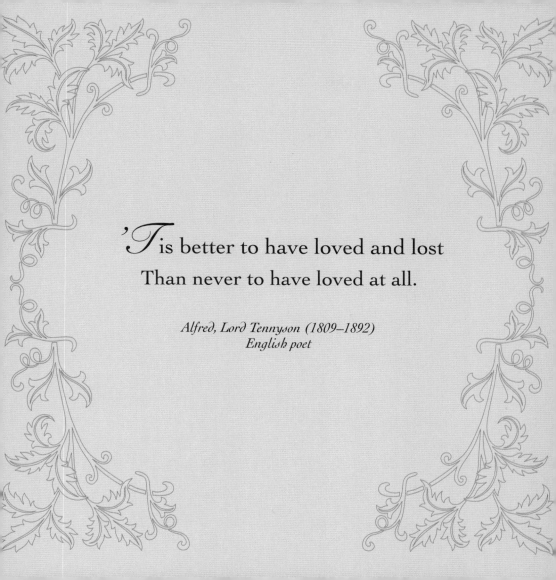

'*T*is better to have loved and lost
Than never to have loved at all.

Alfred, Lord Tennyson (1809–1892)
English poet

Read in these Roses the sad story
Of my hard fate, and your own glory;
In the white you may discover
The paleness of a fainting lover;
In the red the flames still feeding
On my heart with fresh wounds bleeding.
The white will tell you how I languish,
And the red express my anguish,
The white my innocence displaying,
The red my martyrdom betraying;
The frowns that on your brow resided,
Have those roses thus divided.
Oh! let your smiles but clear the weather,
And then they both shall grow together.

Thomas Carew (1594–1639)
English poet

Love is like quicksilver in the hand.
Leave the fingers open and it stays.
Clutch it and it darts away.

Dorothy Parker (1893–1967)
American writer and satirist

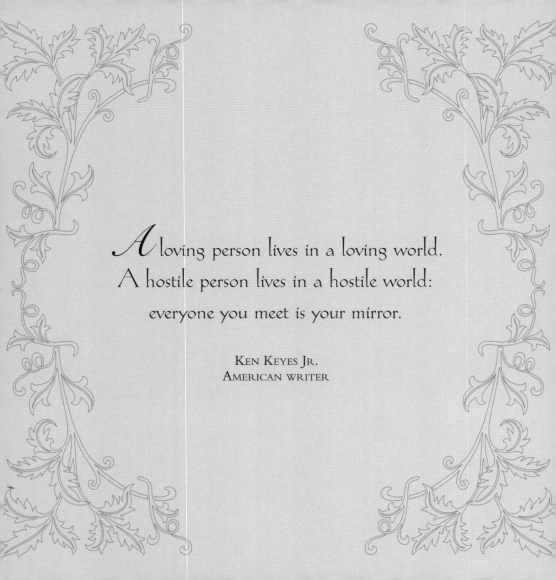

A loving person lives in a loving world.
A hostile person lives in a hostile world:

everyone you meet is your mirror.

KEN KEYES JR.
AMERICAN WRITER

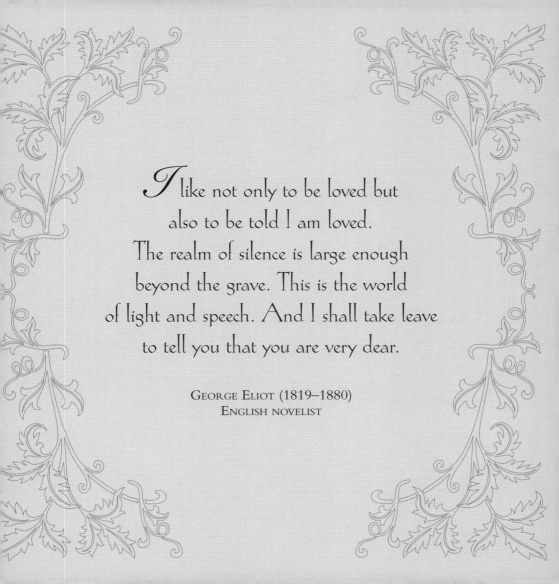

I like not only to be loved but
also to be told I am loved.
The realm of silence is large enough
beyond the grave. This is the world
of light and speech. And I shall take leave
to tell you that you are very dear.

GEORGE ELIOT (1819–1880)
ENGLISH NOVELIST

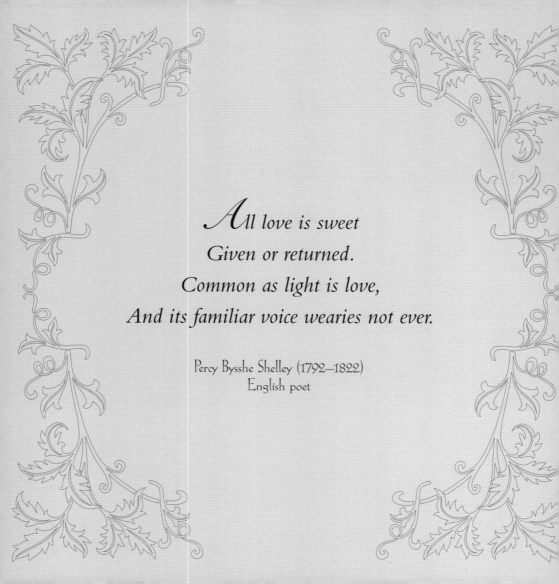

All love is sweet
Given or returned.
Common as light is love,
And its familiar voice wearies not ever.

Percy Bysshe Shelley (1792–1822)
English poet

I Love You

My Sweet Love

The way you love me feels like home.
Just the sound of your voice renews my
strength, as the touch of your hand settles
my soul. Thank you for your open arms,
your acceptance of who I am, and this
limitless freedom my heart finds in yours.
I love you.

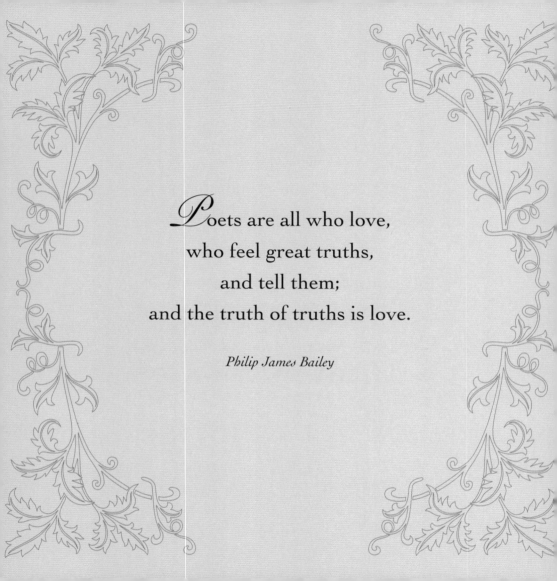

*P*oets are all who love,
who feel great truths,
and tell them;
and the truth of truths is love.

Philip James Bailey

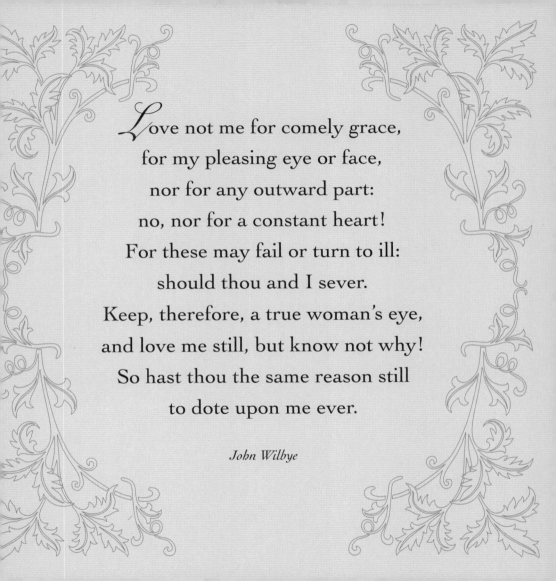

Love not me for comely grace,
for my pleasing eye or face,
nor for any outward part:
no, nor for a constant heart!
For these may fail or turn to ill:
should thou and I sever.
Keep, therefore, a true woman's eye,
and love me still, but know not why!
So hast thou the same reason still
to dote upon me ever.

John Wilbye

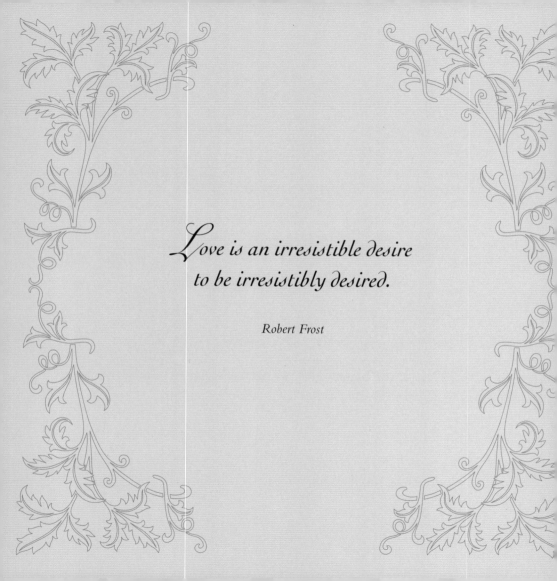

*Love is an irresistible desire
to be irresistibly desired.*

Robert Frost

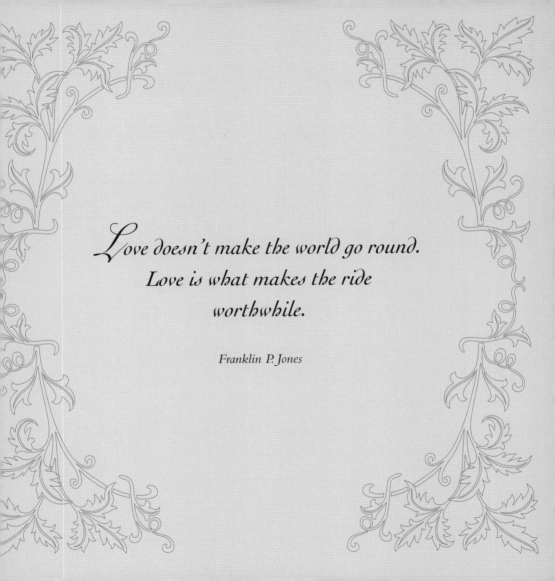

Love doesn't make the world go round.
Love is what makes the ride
worthwhile.

Franklin P. Jones

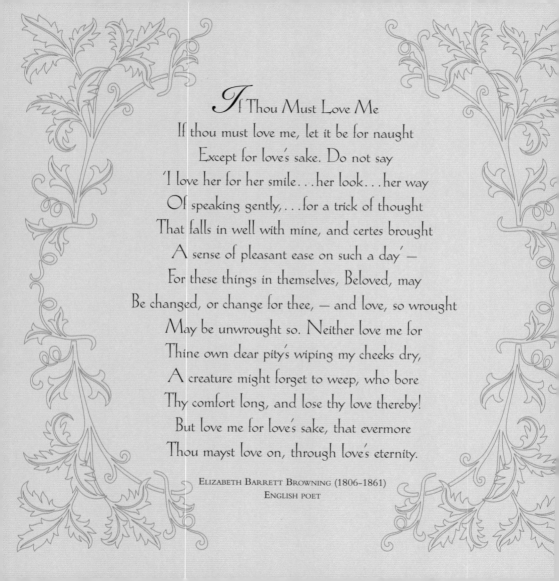

If Thou Must Love Me

If thou must love me, let it be for naught
Except for love's sake. Do not say
'I love her for her smile...her look...her way
Of speaking gently,...for a trick of thought
That falls in well with mine, and certes brought
A sense of pleasant ease on such a day' —
For these things in themselves, Beloved, may
Be changed, or change for thee, — and love, so wrought
May be unwrought so. Neither love me for
Thine own dear pity's wiping my cheeks dry,
A creature might forget to weep, who bore
Thy comfort long, and lose thy love thereby!
But love me for love's sake, that evermore
Thou mayst love on, through love's eternity.

ELIZABETH BARRETT BROWNING (1806–1861)
ENGLISH POET

$\mathcal{T}$o love is to receive a glimpse of heaven.

KAREN SUNDE

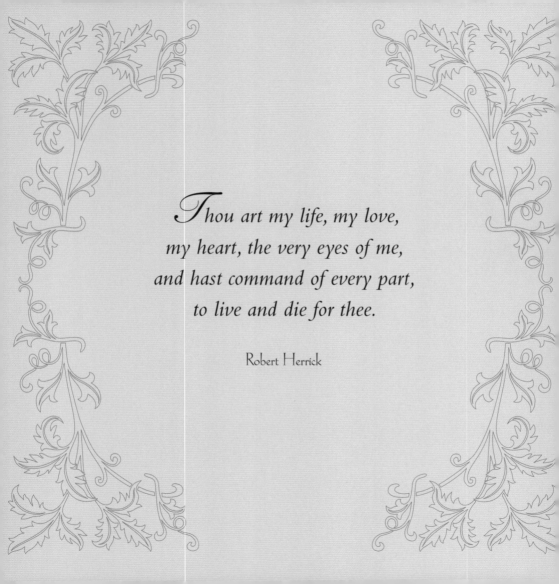

Thou art my life, my love,
my heart, the very eyes of me,
and hast command of every part,
to live and die for thee.

Robert Herrick

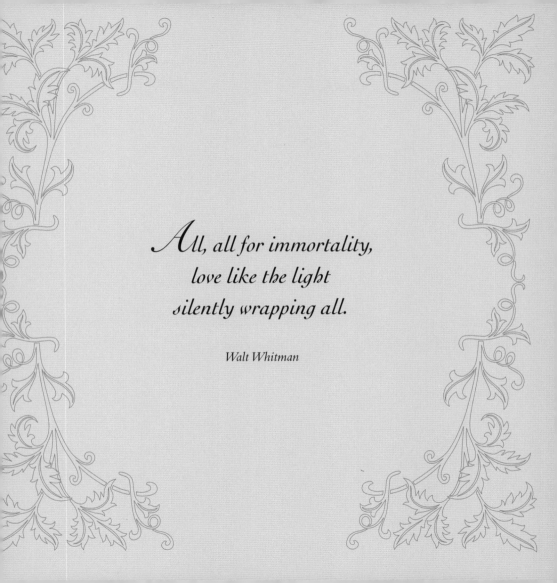

All, all for immortality,
love like the light
silently wrapping all.

Walt Whitman

$\mathcal{G}$od, from a beautiful necessity,
is love.

MARTIN FARQUHAR TUPPER

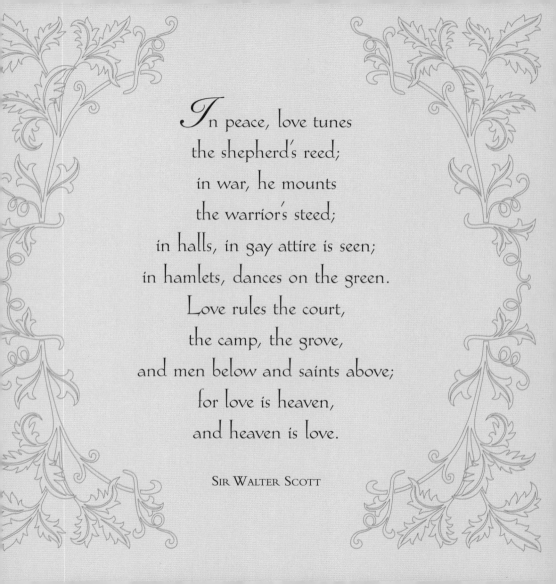

In peace, love tunes
the shepherd's reed;
in war, he mounts
the warrior's steed;
in halls, in gay attire is seen;
in hamlets, dances on the green.
Love rules the court,
the camp, the grove,
and men below and saints above;
for love is heaven,
and heaven is love.

SIR WALTER SCOTT

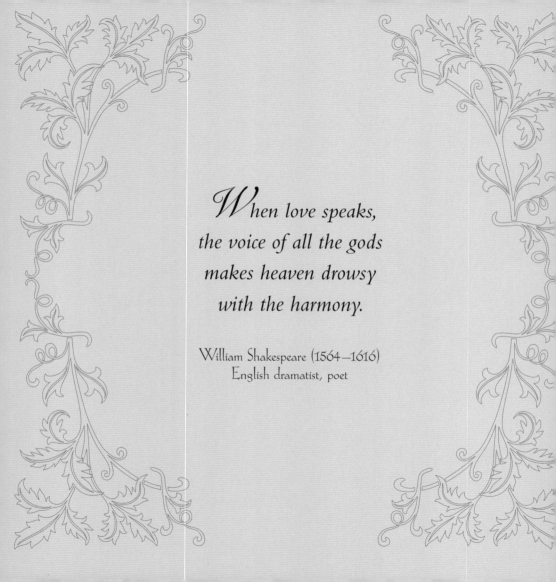

When love speaks,
the voice of all the gods
makes heaven drowsy
with the harmony.

William Shakespeare (1564–1616)
English dramatist, poet

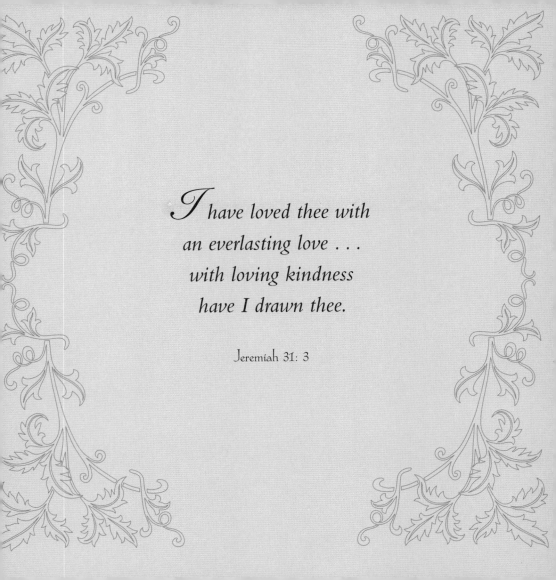

I have loved thee with
an everlasting love . . .
with loving kindness
have I drawn thee.

Jeremiah 31: 3

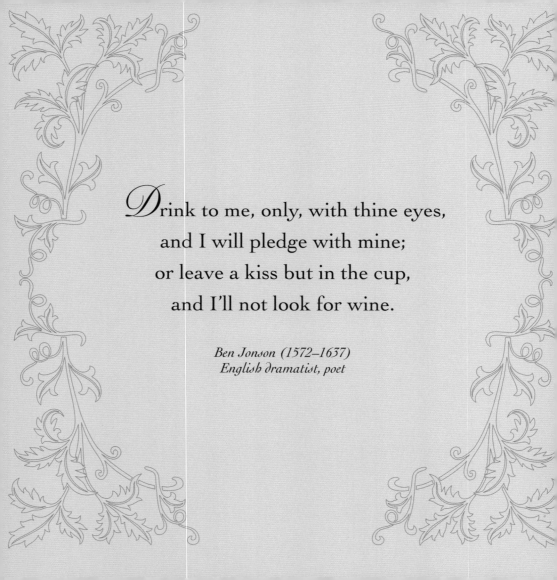

Drink to me, only, with thine eyes,
and I will pledge with mine;
or leave a kiss but in the cup,
and I'll not look for wine.

Ben Jonson (1572–1637)
English dramatist, poet

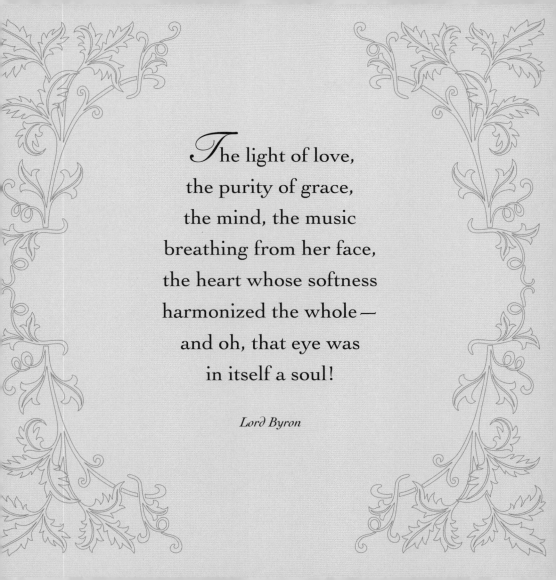

The light of love,
the purity of grace,
the mind, the music
breathing from her face,
the heart whose softness
harmonized the whole—
and oh, that eye was
in itself a soul!

Lord Byron

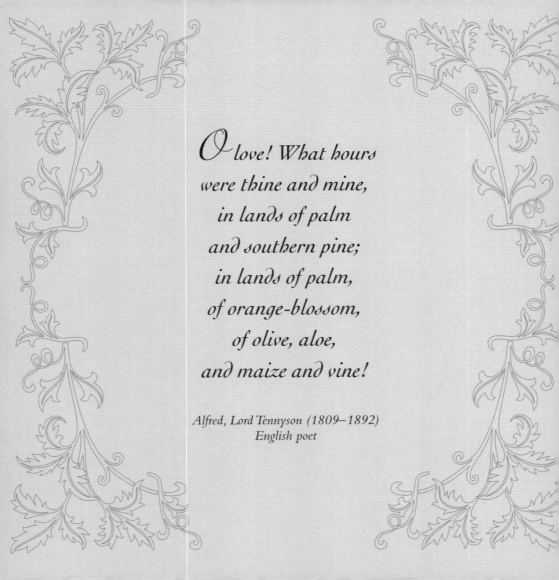

*O love! What hours
were thine and mine,
in lands of palm
and southern pine;
in lands of palm,
of orange-blossom,
of olive, aloe,
and maize and vine!*

Alfred, Lord Tennyson (1809–1892)
English poet

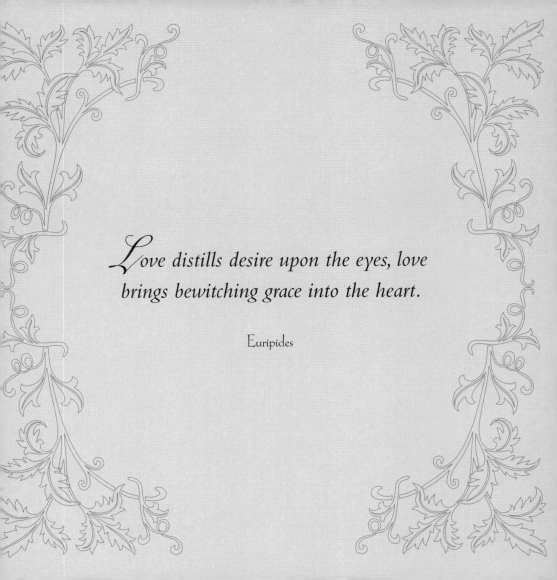

*Love distills desire upon the eyes, love
brings bewitching grace into the heart.*

Euripides

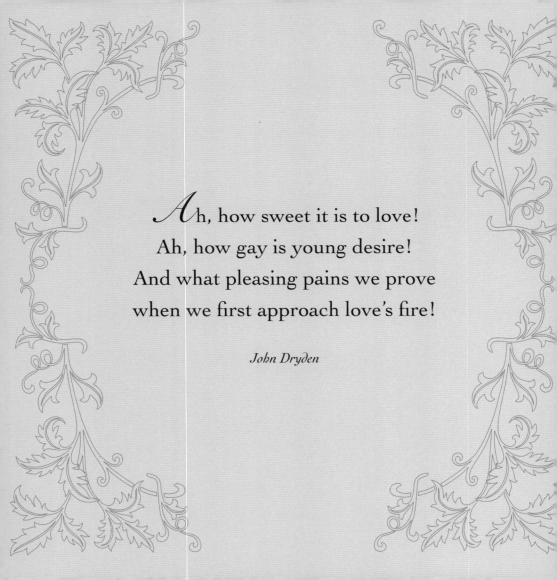

$\mathcal{A}$h, how sweet it is to love!
Ah, how gay is young desire!
And what pleasing pains we prove
when we first approach love's fire!

John Dryden

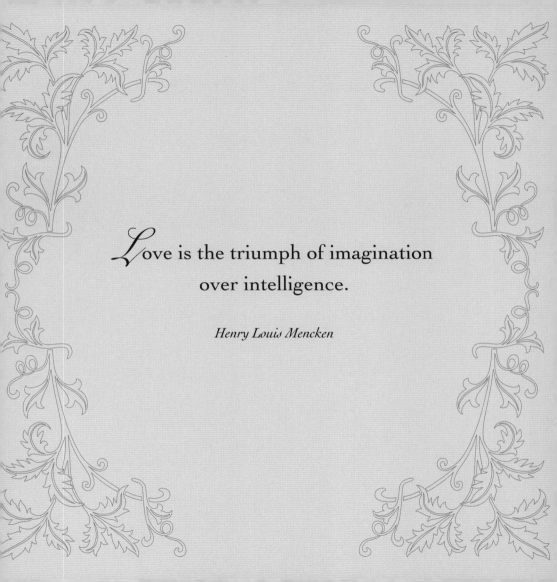

$\mathcal{L}$ove is the triumph of imagination
over intelligence.

Henry Louis Mencken

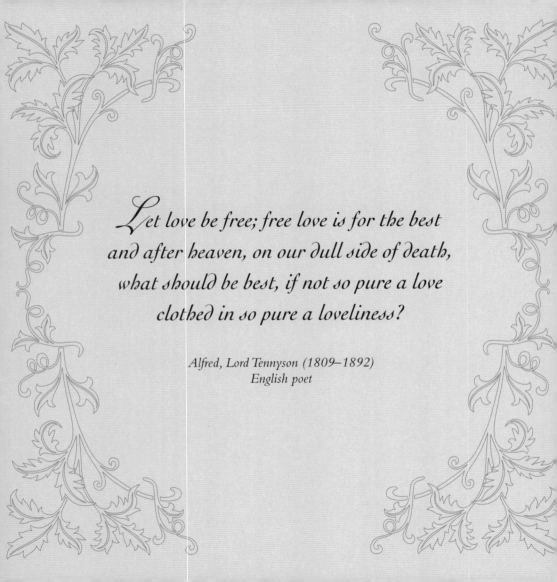

Let love be free; free love is for the best
and after heaven, on our dull side of death,
what should be best, if not so pure a love
clothed in so pure a loveliness?

Alfred, Lord Tennyson (1809–1892)
English poet

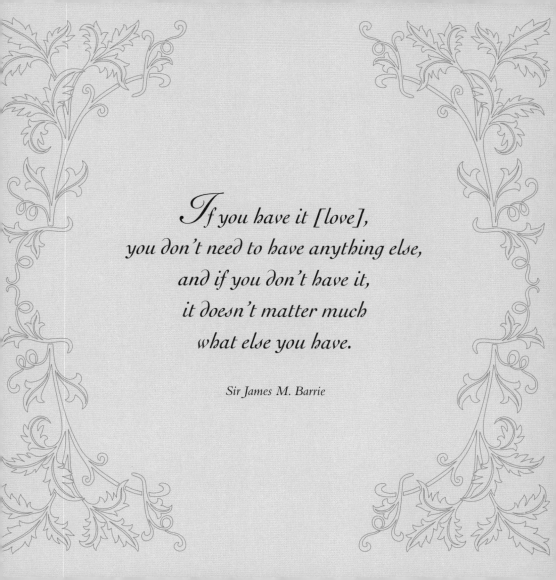

If you have it [love],
you don't need to have anything else,
and if you don't have it,
it doesn't matter much
what else you have.

Sir James M. Barrie

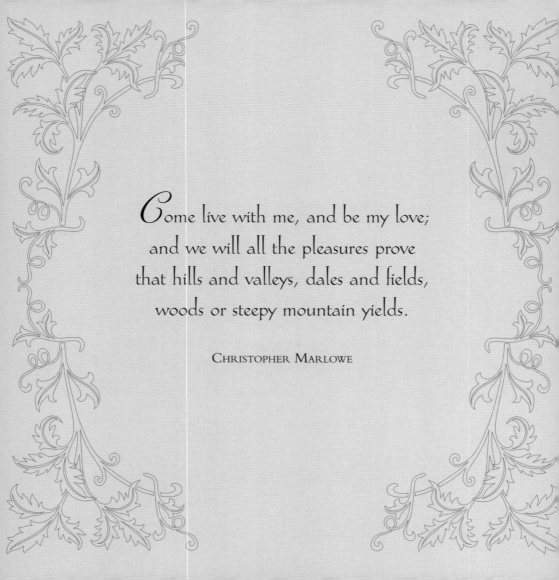

Come live with me, and be my love;
and we will all the pleasures prove
that hills and valleys, dales and fields,
woods or steepy mountain yields.

CHRISTOPHER MARLOWE

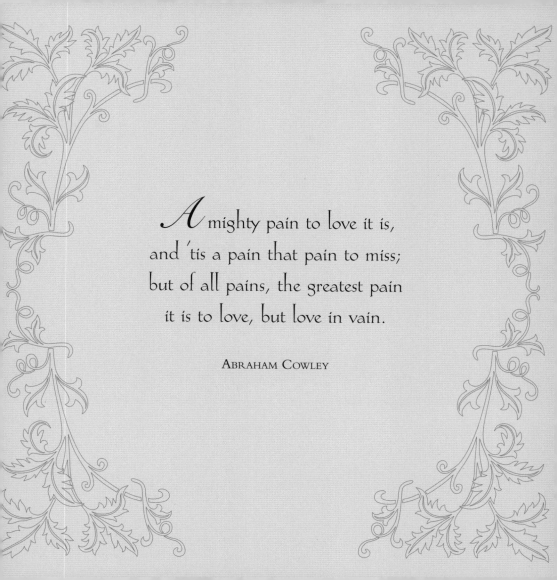

A mighty pain to love it is,
and 'tis a pain that pain to miss;
but of all pains, the greatest pain
it is to love, but love in vain.

ABRAHAM COWLEY

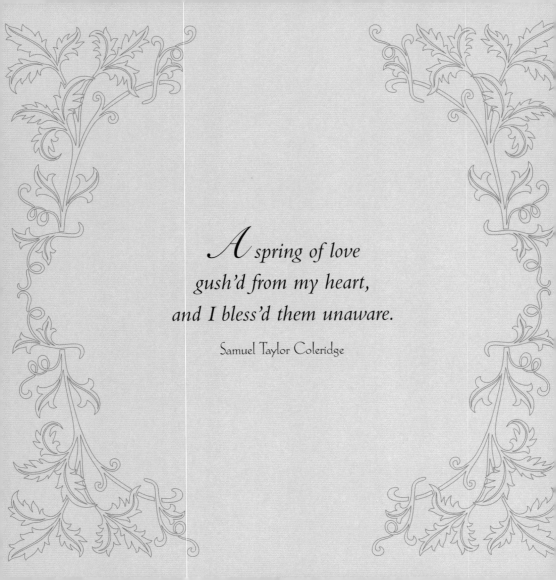

A spring of love
gush'd from my heart,
and I bless'd them unaware.

Samuel Taylor Coleridge

$\mathcal{L}$ove is friendship set to music.

E. Joseph Cossman

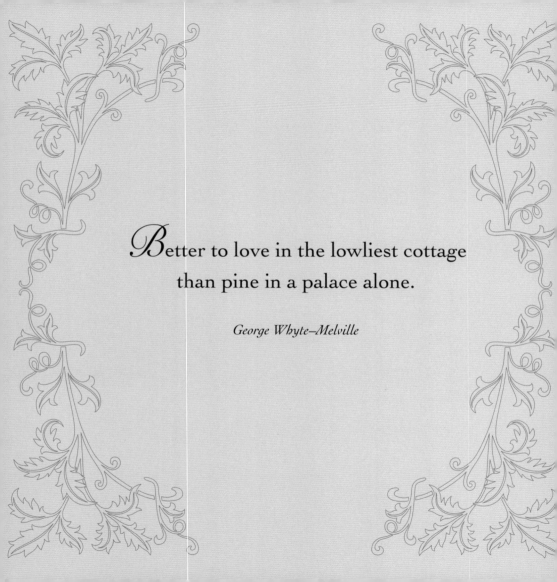

$\mathcal{B}$etter to love in the lowliest cottage
than pine in a palace alone.

George Whyte–Melville

*L*et them also that love thy name
be joyful in thee.

Psalm 5:11

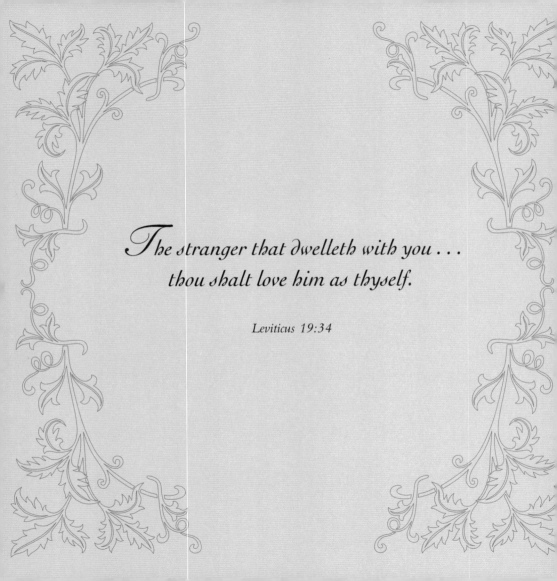

*The stranger that dwelleth with you . . .
thou shalt love him as thyself.*

Leviticus 19:34

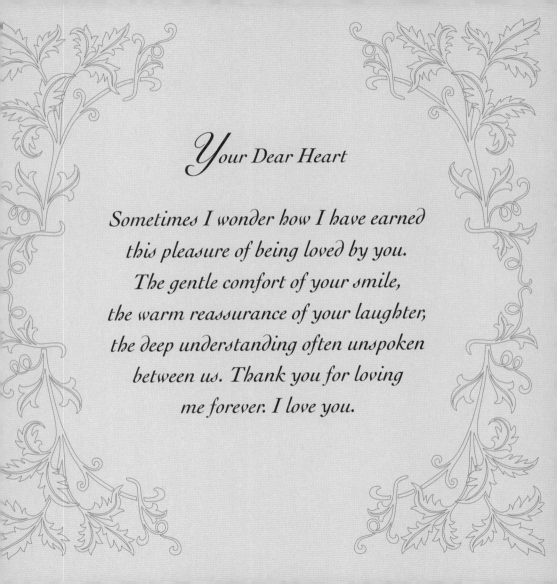

Your Dear Heart

*Sometimes I wonder how I have earned
this pleasure of being loved by you.
The gentle comfort of your smile,
the warm reassurance of your laughter,
the deep understanding often unspoken
between us. Thank you for loving
me forever. I love you.*

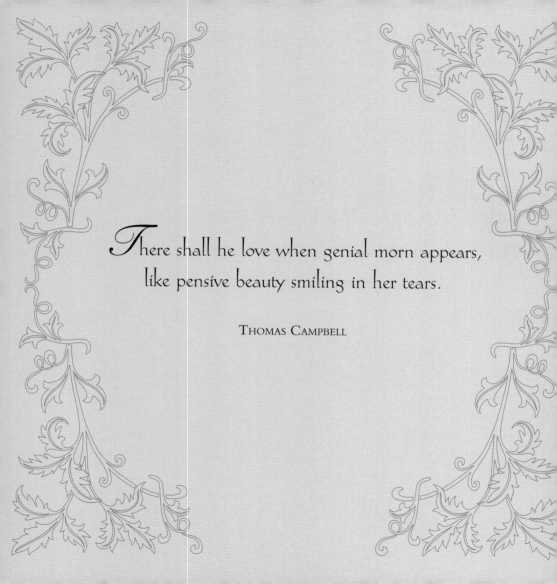

There shall he love when genial morn appears,
like pensive beauty smiling in her tears.

THOMAS CAMPBELL

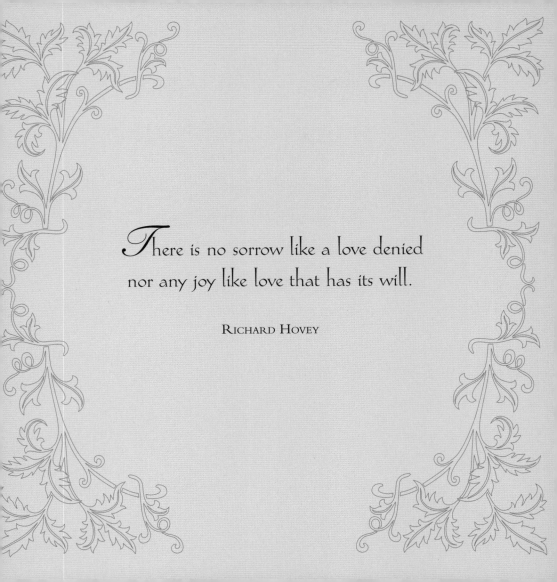

There is no sorrow like a love denied
nor any joy like love that has its will.

RICHARD HOVEY

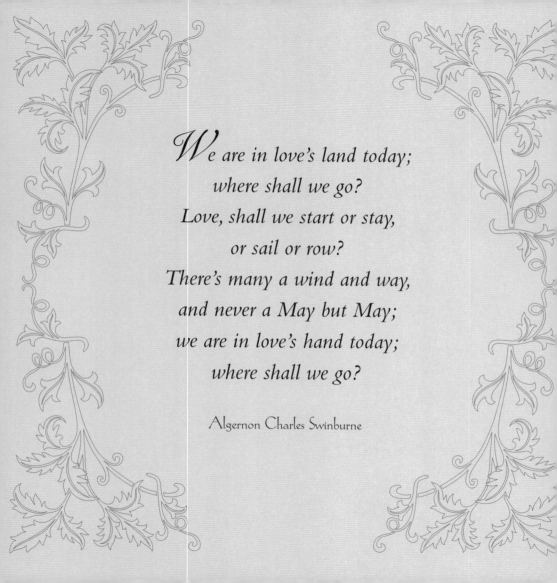

We are in love's land today;
where shall we go?
Love, shall we start or stay,
or sail or row?
There's many a wind and way,
and never a May but May;
we are in love's hand today;
where shall we go?

Algernon Charles Swinburne

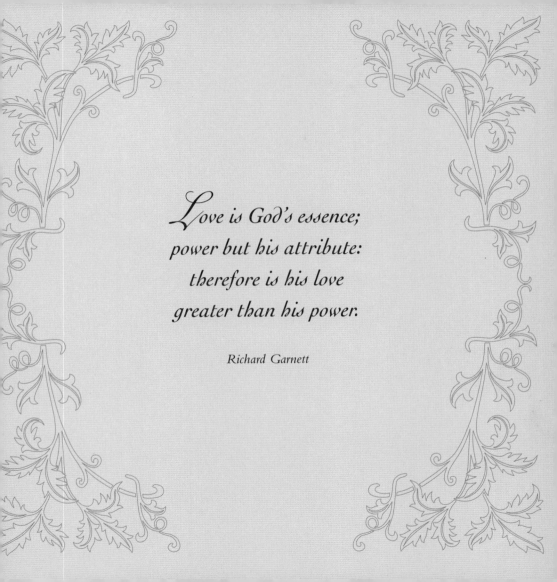

*Love is God's essence;
power but his attribute:
therefore is his love
greater than his power.*

Richard Garnett

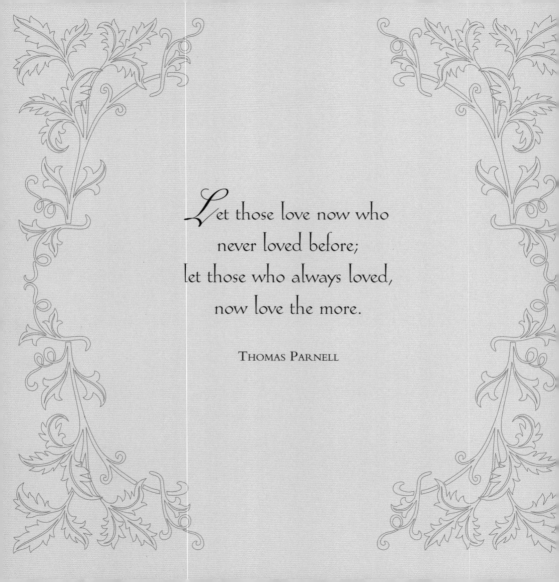

Let those love now who
never loved before;
let those who always loved,
now love the more.

THOMAS PARNELL

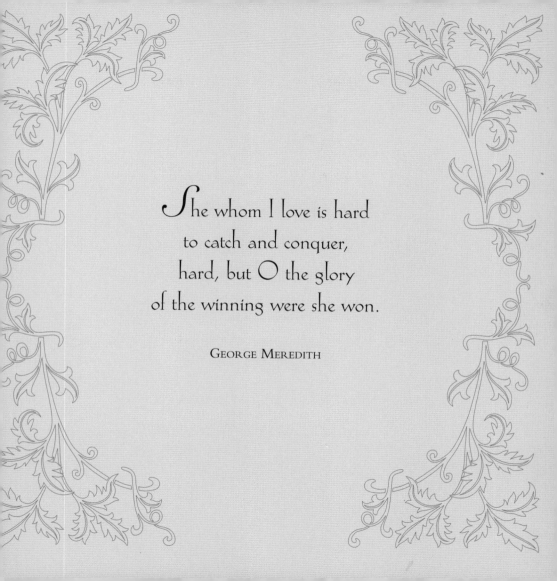

She whom I love is hard
to catch and conquer,
hard, but O the glory
of the winning were she won.

GEORGE MEREDITH

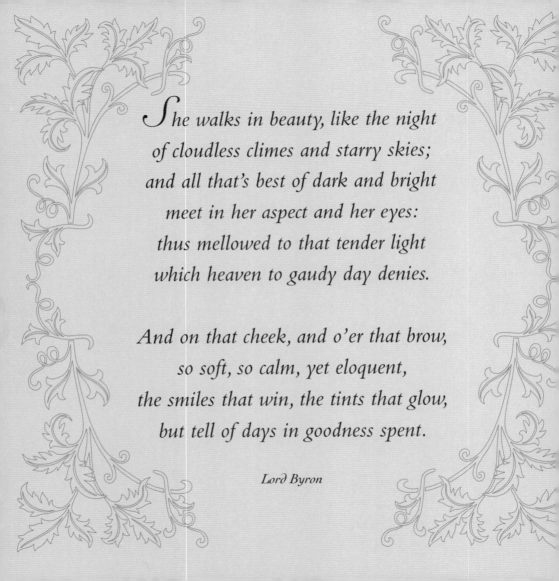

She walks in beauty, like the night
of cloudless climes and starry skies;
and all that's best of dark and bright
meet in her aspect and her eyes:
thus mellowed to that tender light
which heaven to gaudy day denies.

And on that cheek, and o'er that brow,
so soft, so calm, yet eloquent,
the smiles that win, the tints that glow,
but tell of days in goodness spent.

Lord Byron

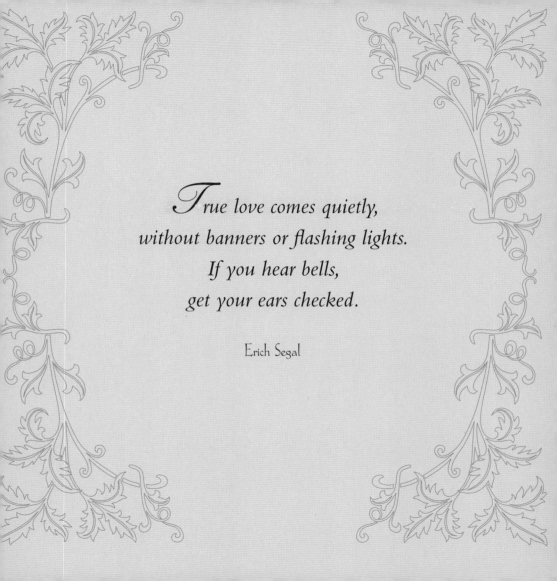

True love comes quietly,
without banners or flashing lights.
If you hear bells,
get your ears checked.

Erich Segal

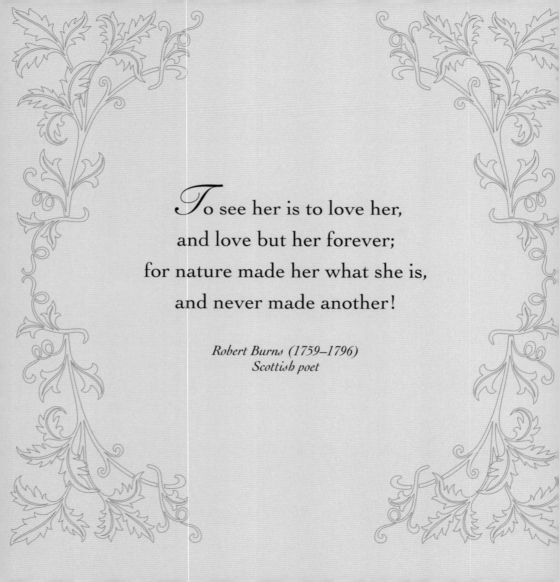

To see her is to love her,
and love but her forever;
for nature made her what she is,
and never made another!

Robert Burns (1759–1796)
Scottish poet

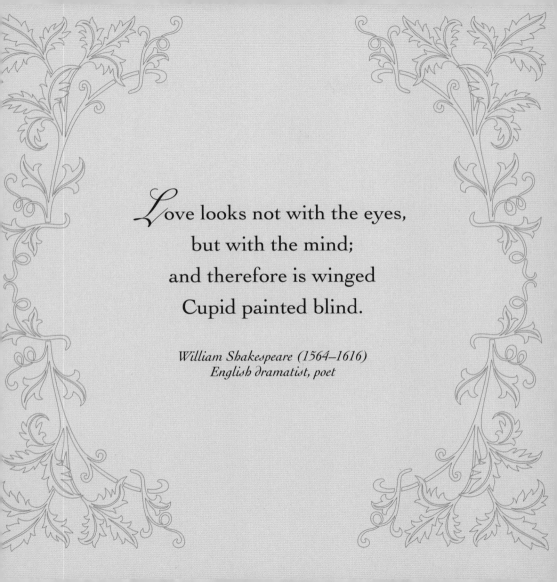

$\mathcal{L}$ove looks not with the eyes,
but with the mind;
and therefore is winged
Cupid painted blind.

William Shakespeare (1564–1616)
English dramatist, poet

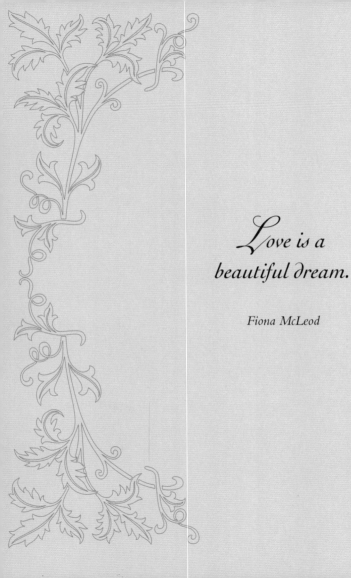

Love is a
beautiful dream.

Fiona McLeod

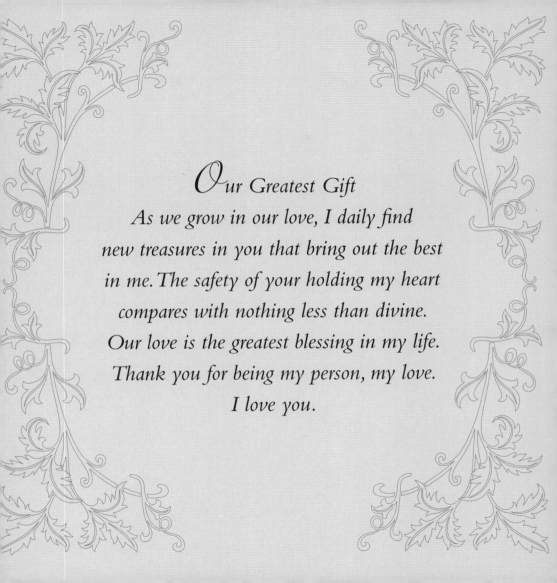

Our Greatest Gift

*As we grow in our love, I daily find
new treasures in you that bring out the best
in me. The safety of your holding my heart
compares with nothing less than divine.
Our love is the greatest blessing in my life.
Thank you for being my person, my love.
I love you.*

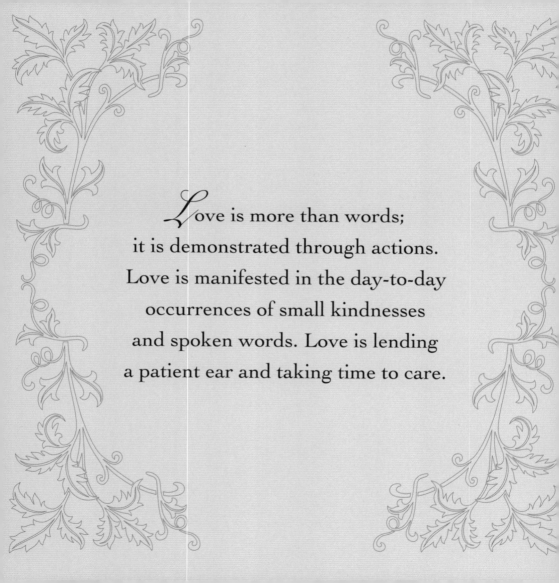

Love is more than words;
it is demonstrated through actions.
Love is manifested in the day-to-day
occurrences of small kindnesses
and spoken words. Love is lending
a patient ear and taking time to care.

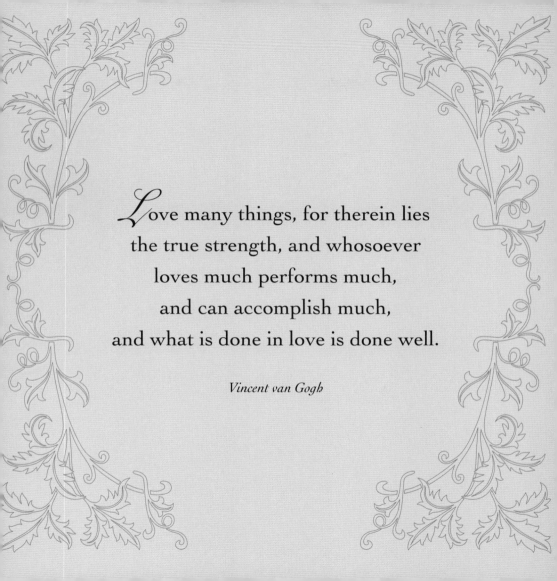

*L*ove many things, for therein lies
the true strength, and whosoever
loves much performs much,
and can accomplish much,
and what is done in love is done well.

Vincent van Gogh

Love is the enchanted dawn of every heart.

Alphonse Marie de la Martine

*Pains of love be sweeter far
than all other pleasures are.*

John Dryden

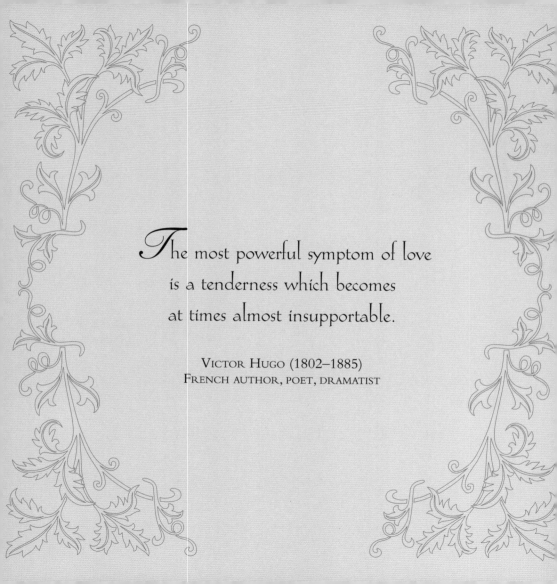

The most powerful symptom of love
is a tenderness which becomes
at times almost insupportable.

VICTOR HUGO (1802–1885)
FRENCH AUTHOR, POET, DRAMATIST

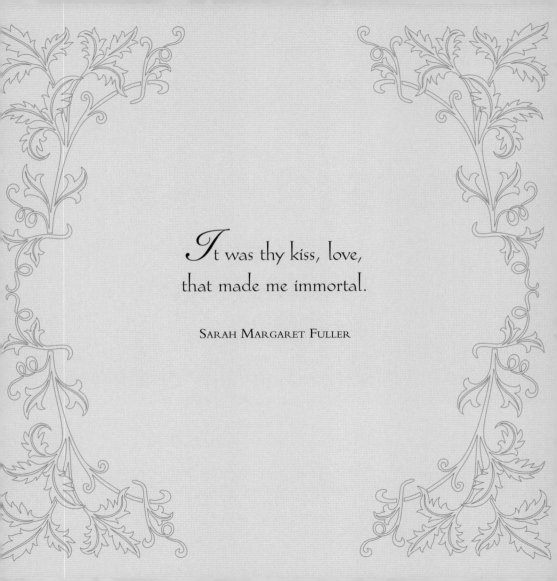

*I*t was thy kiss, love,
that made me immortal.

SARAH MARGARET FULLER

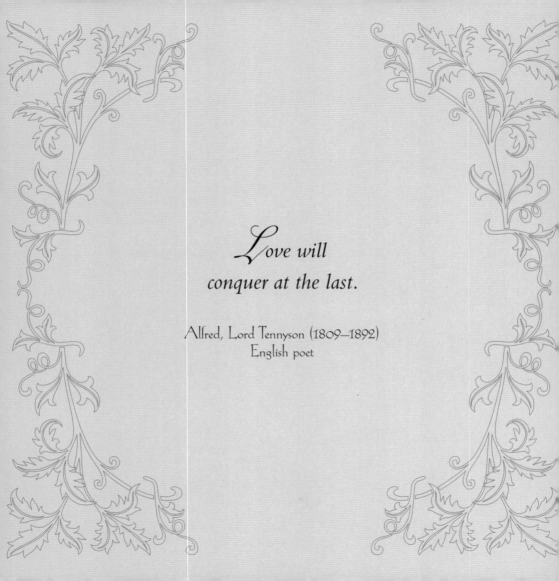

$\mathcal{L}$ove will
conquer at the last.

Alfred, Lord Tennyson (1809–1892)
English poet

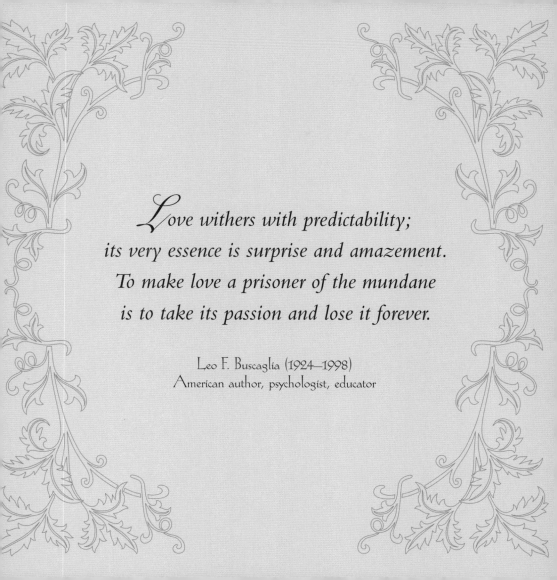

Love withers with predictability;
its very essence is surprise and amazement.
To make love a prisoner of the mundane
is to take its passion and lose it forever.

Leo F. Buscaglia (1924–1998)
American author, psychologist, educator

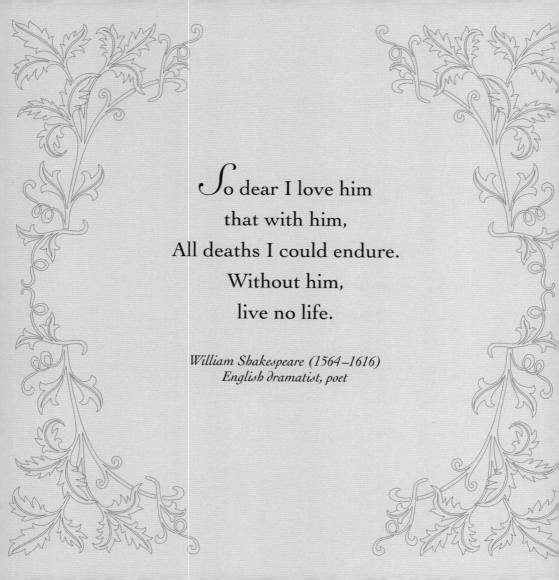

So dear I love him
that with him,
All deaths I could endure.
Without him,
live no life.

William Shakespeare (1564–1616)
English dramatist, poet

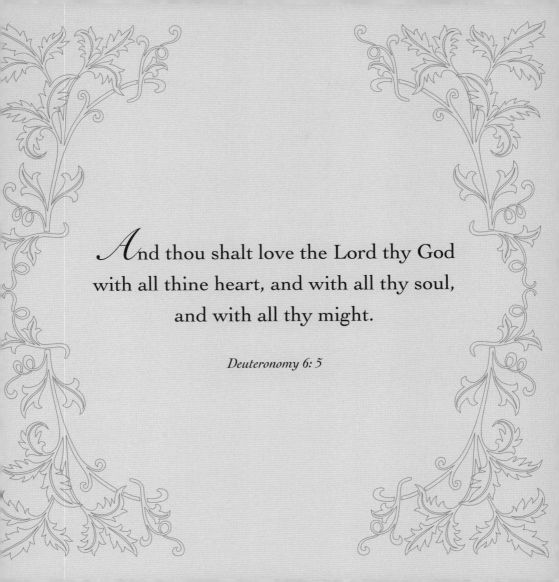

And thou shalt love the Lord thy God
with all thine heart, and with all thy soul,
and with all thy might.

Deuteronomy 6: 5

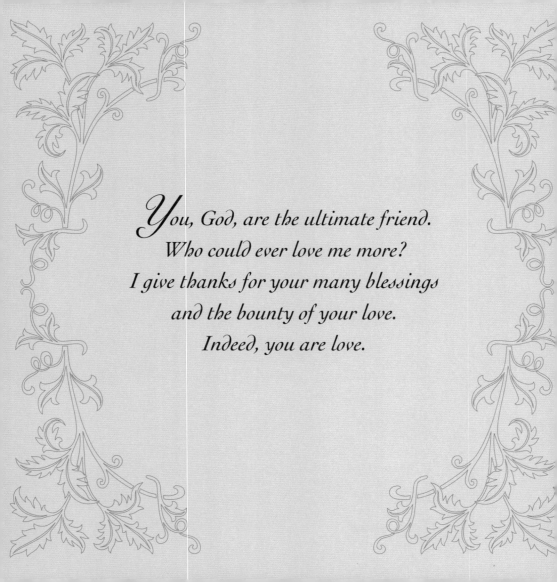

You, God, are the ultimate friend.
Who could ever love me more?
I give thanks for your many blessings
and the bounty of your love.
Indeed, you are love.

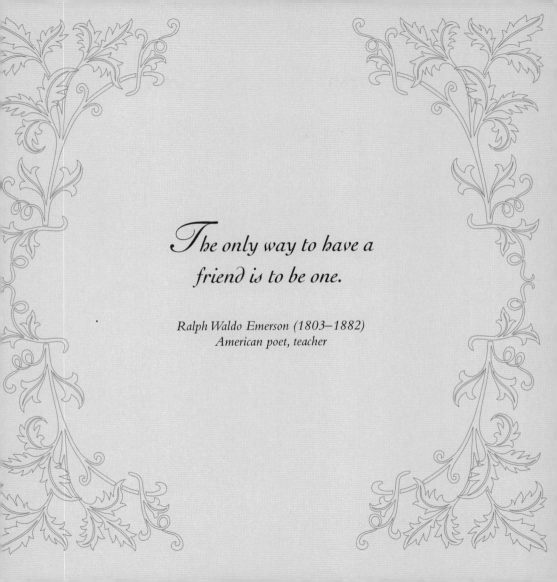

The only way to have a friend is to be one.

Ralph Waldo Emerson (1803–1882)
American poet, teacher

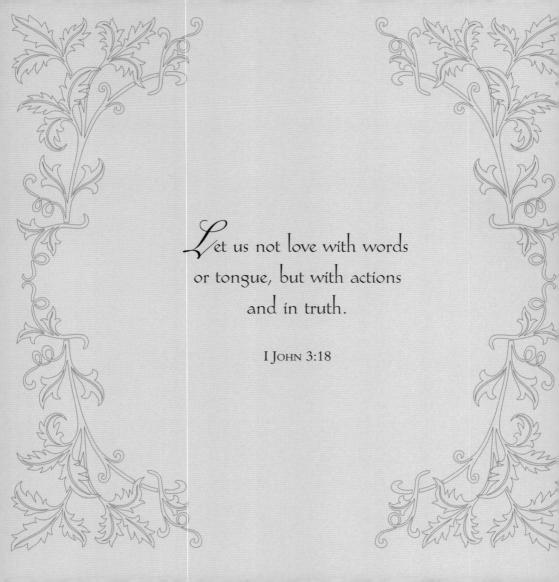

$\mathcal{L}$et us not love with words
or tongue, but with actions
and in truth.

I JOHN 3:18

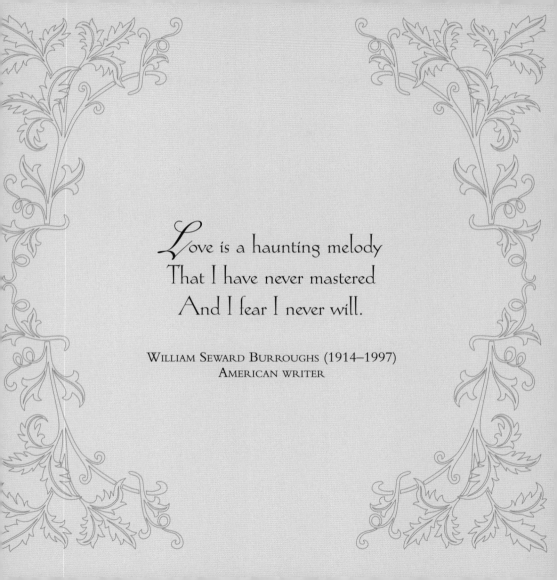

*L*ove is a haunting melody
That I have never mastered
And I fear I never will.

WILLIAM SEWARD BURROUGHS (1914–1997)
AMERICAN WRITER

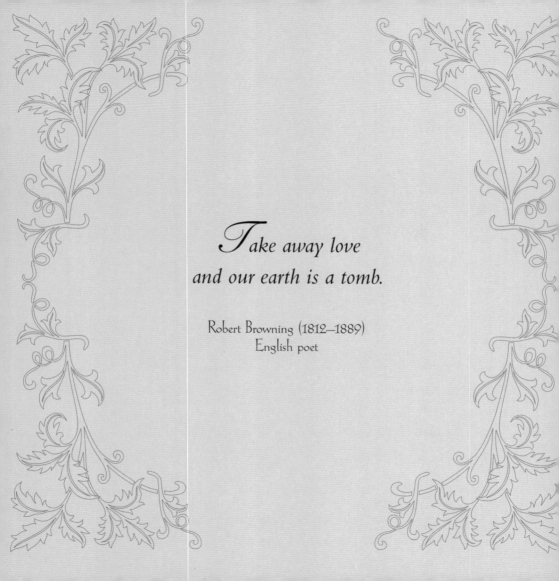

*Take away love
and our earth is a tomb.*

Robert Browning (1812–1889)
English poet

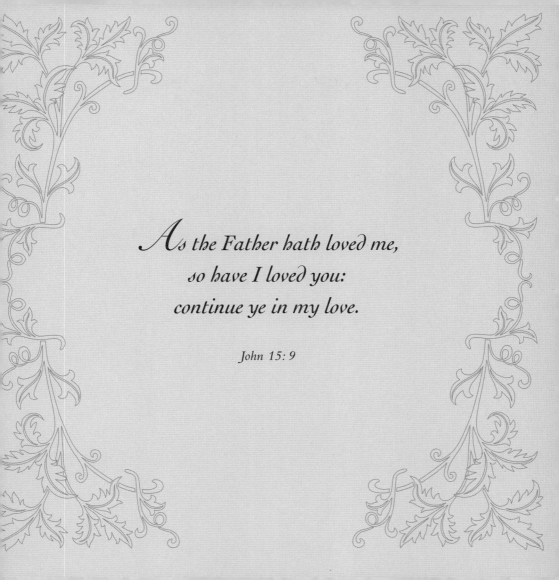

As the Father hath loved me,
so have I loved you:
continue ye in my love.

John 15: 9

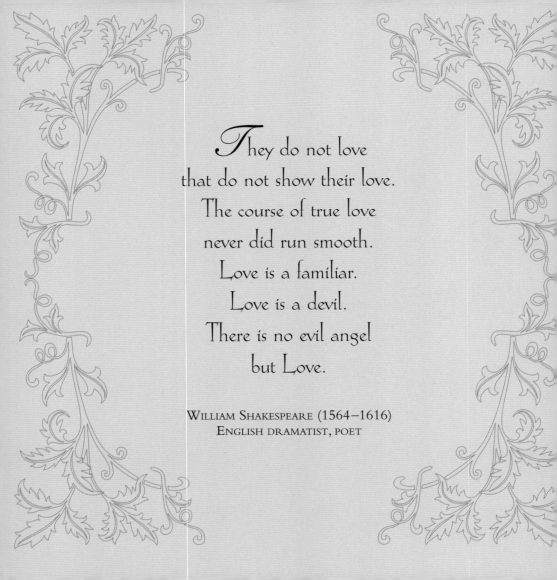

They do not love
that do not show their love.
The course of true love
never did run smooth.
Love is a familiar.
Love is a devil.
There is no evil angel
but Love.

WILLIAM SHAKESPEARE (1564–1616)
ENGLISH DRAMATIST, POET

BEST OF
SPA DESIGN

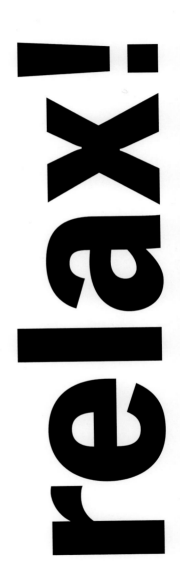

Imprint

The Deutsche Nationalbibliothek lists this publication in the Deutsche Nationalbibliografie;
detailed bibliographical data are available on the internet at http://dnb.d-nb.de.

ISBN 978-3-03768-057-5
© 2010 by Braun Publishing AG
www.braun-publishing.ch

2nd edition 2010

Editorial staff: Annika Schulz
Translation: Stephen Roche, Hamburg
Graphic concept: Michaela Prinz

BEST OF
SPA DESIGN

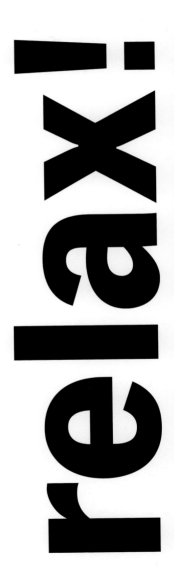

relax!

BRAUN

6	**Preface**		108	**Health Center Lanserhof** D E SIGNSTUDIO Regina Dahmen-Ingenhoven
10	**Amayana Spa** Hennings Börn Interiors		120	**Hints** Giampaolo Benedini Architects
16	**Ansitz Endrici** monovolume		130	**Hotel de France** Grassl Haertwig Architekten
22	**Bathhouse** Richardson Sadeki		138	**Hotel Q** Graft – Gesellschaft von Architekten mbH
34	**Bathroom in Velp** Dirkjan Broekhuizen Interieurarchitect BNI			
42	**Club Sportive** PrastHooft		146	**Kaufman Loft Bath** Studio Rinaldi
50	**DeWispelaere** Venlet Interior Architecture bvba		152	**Kinuta Stone Spa** Megumi Matsubara & Hiroi Ariyama
58	**The Dome** G. Hakan Kulahci		158	**Kusaba Apartment** Takao Shiotsuka Atelier
68	**Dornbracht Elemental Spa** Meiré und Meiré		166	**La Réserve Genève Hotel & Spa** Jacques Garcia
78	**Espace Payot** Joseph Caspari		174	**Labo Day Spa** Aroma Productions AG
88	**Geleen Bath** Otello Gatto		180	**Liquidrom** gmp – Architekten von Gerkan, Marg und Partner
98	**Hamam Trafo** integrales Planungsteam ushitamborriello, Innenar- chitektur & Szenenbild		190	**Lofthouse** Crepain Binst Architecture

200 **Loft Bathroom**
BUB architekten

210 **Lute Suites**
Marcel Wanders Studio

222 **McCarthy Residence**
stephen varady architecture

226 **Mill House**
Wingårdh

236 **Moku Moku Yu**
Klein Dytham architecture

246 **Penthouse**
Private Bathing Area
kramer biwer mau
architekten

252 **Private Bathing Area**
Acquaplan

262 **Private Bathroom**
Loodszeven
Interieurarchitecten

270 **Puls 5**
ushitamborriello Innen-
architektur & Szenenbild
Oberholzer & Brüschweiler
Architekten

280 **Refurbishment of a**
Bathroom
SEITEN_ANSICHT

286 **Regatta Condominium**
Leopoldo Rosati
Architecture

294 **Residence on a Hill**
lohrmannarchitekt

306 **Residential Building**
Axel Nieberg

314 **Rubin Residence**
McIntosh Poris Associates

320 **Silver Rain a La Prairie Spa**
Carl D'Aquino & Francine
Monaco of D'Aquino Monaco

328 **Spa Barn**
Nalbach + Nalbach
Hon. Prof. Johanne
Nalbach

336 **Spa Wolfsburg**
Büro Wehberg

346 **Then?**
N Maeda Atelier

354 **Thermal Spa**
Behnisch Architekten

368 **Tschuggen Bergoase**
Mario Botta

380 **Wellnesspark ELSE-Club**
4a Architekten

388 **Yi Spa**
plajer & franz studio

398 Architects Index

400 Picture Credits

Preface

There are social trends that are quickly reflected in the prevailing architectural style. The new joy of cooking, for example, has led to kitchens being increasingly designed as open spaces today. Within the past few years, a rethinking process took place in this area that substantially altered the view of a functional part of the home. In the bathroom sector a similar trend seems to be taking place that is expected to increase in the near future. The interesting aspect of this trend is the correlation between public and private bathing areas. This is mainly the reason why the fashionable term SPA has become the synonym for restorative relaxation – increasingly also in the privacy of the home.

However, the frequently stated belief that the word spa is a Latin acronym – sanus per aquam (health through water) – is only an illusion since neither the sources nor the rules of Latin grammar support such a conclusion. Instead the symbolic value of the word actually derives from the Belgian bathing resort of Spa, which was already frequented by British tourists in the 16th century. Yet antiquity is an interesting starting point for studying the culture of bathing. The Roman Thermae were public places and water a precious commodity that was fetched via aqueducts. The link between hygiene and sufficient water supply was one of the basic pillars of the imperium romanum. In the Middle Ages, public bath houses were the place in which most people came in contact with running water. Crusaders had brought the concept and the construction plans along with them from the Middle East. However, re-

ligious prudery, the spread of syphilis and, last but not least, the great bubonic plague epidemics resulted in the shutting down of most bath houses. From then on, especially among feudal circles, personal hygiene was reduced to the use of perfumes.

It was not until the 19th century that new hygienic insights led to a revival of public baths. This was followed by the increased privatization of baths. Gaining in strength, the bourgeoisie added bathrooms as a representative architectural element to their homes, creating a new functional room. Until the period of promoterism many urban houses at least featured a common bathroom in the hallway. Individualization progressed as people were now eager to construct a separate bathroom in each residential unit. Those who had plenty of space at their disposal even managed to install a guest toilet or guest bathroom. This progressed into the assignment of separate bathing areas to each person in the household, where possible. Whether the efforts include installing master bathrooms, parent and children bathrooms or simple dual bathroom sinks, all have one aim in common – turning the bathroom into an individual area of expression and retreat. This way, in its architectural evolution from a public to a private space, the bathroom developed into the perfect symbol of cocooning.

As a result of the recent wellness movement, an exciting observation can be made at this point. Increasingly, public bathing institutions that for a long time only drudged along as boring swimming halls are gaining in popularity. Spruced up by architects and designers, they shine as new spa temples that not only revive the ritual character of bathing during antiquity, but also include Middle Eastern and oriental influences. This way, they not only define a new public function for the bathing space but also act as ideals and models for the design of many private bathrooms.

Bathrooms in homes increasingly feature an open design while the choice of materials has expanded. The bathroom as a space is given more importance in the planning stage. Previously, bathrooms were frequently located on the interior, while today daylight illumination is almost compulsory. The number of manufacturers of bathroom furniture, faucets and ceramics is also constantly increasing. New materials and manufacturing techniques allow, for example, the use of tiles with unusual dimensions or sinks made of composite materials that can be molded in any shape. This way, they once again constitute cultic vessels for the matter whose specific characteristics enable life on earth – water. At 0° Celsius it turns into ice, at 4° it reaches its highest liquid density – a characteristics that not only ensures the survival of fish. Hot-blooded, our body temperature is around 37°, and finally at 100°, water evaporates into steam.

Far-Eastern motifs combined with **selected** materials create a **peaceful** atmosphere

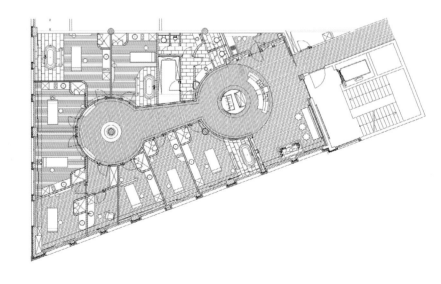

An **open design** combined with a **freestanding** element have created a **bathroom** that is **spacious yet simple**

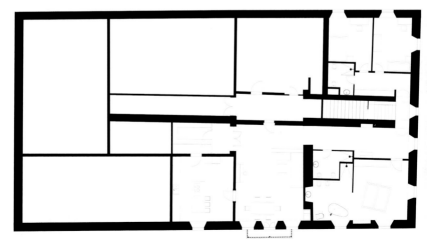

BATHHOUSE

Privacy and **secrecy** are **combined** with an **open landscape** of **water** in all forms

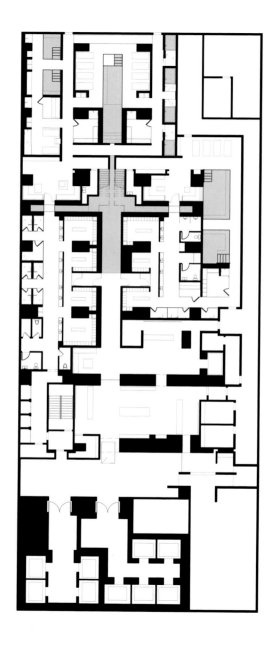

CHILDREN 12 YEARS OF AGE
OR YOUNGER MUST BE
ACCOMPANIED BY AN ADULT.
THE MAXIMUM RECOMMENDED
TIME FOR SUCH CHILDREN TO
USE THE SPA IS 10 MINUTES.

CAPACITY   DIAL 911   CAUTION

17 MAXIMUM NUMBER OF PEOPLE
ALLOWED IN THE SPA AT ONE TIME

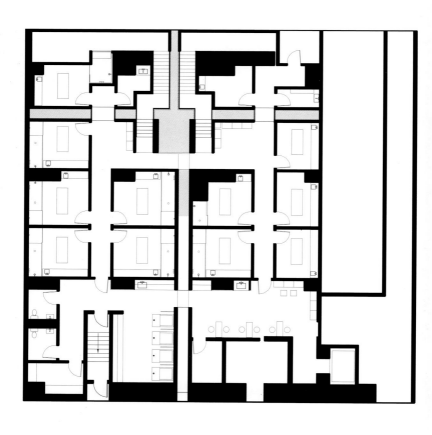

Creating an atmosphere of tranquility

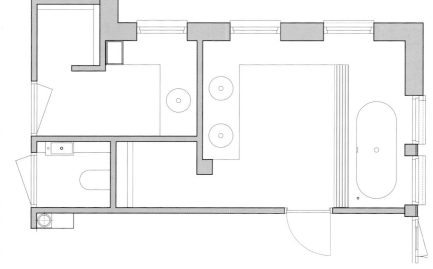

Stucco, cement panels, wallpaper and **wood** provide **distinct** individual atmospheres

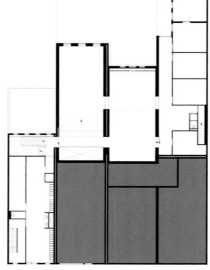

DeWispelaere l Herne l Venlet Interior Architecture bvba

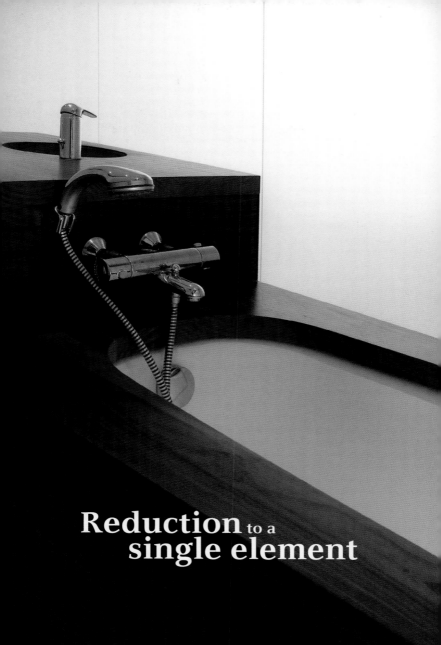

Reduction to a
single element

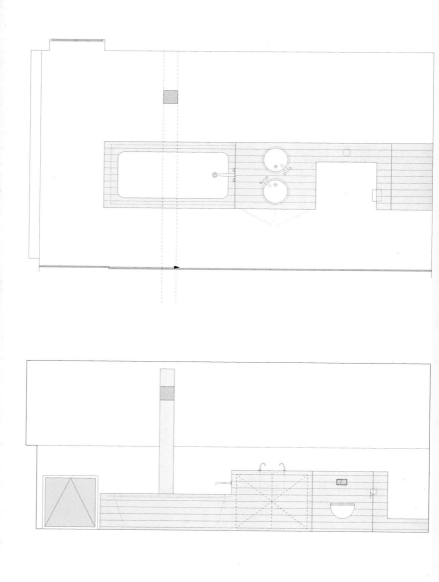

A **colorful** installation to
relax body and **soul**

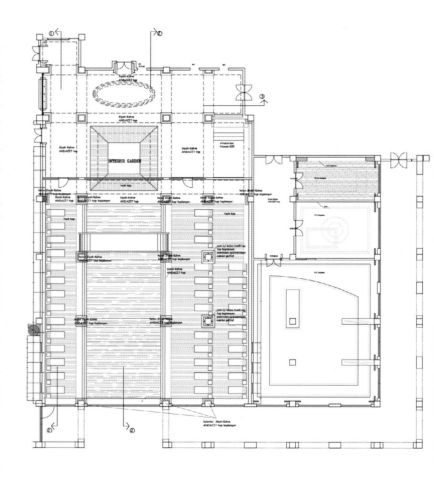

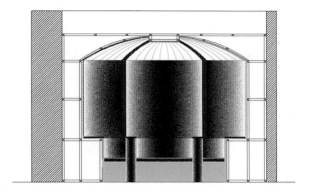

A-A KESİT

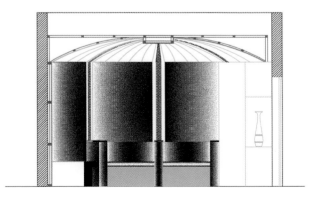

B-B KESİT

68 | **Dornbracht Elemental Spa** | Frankfurt / Main | Meiré und Meiré

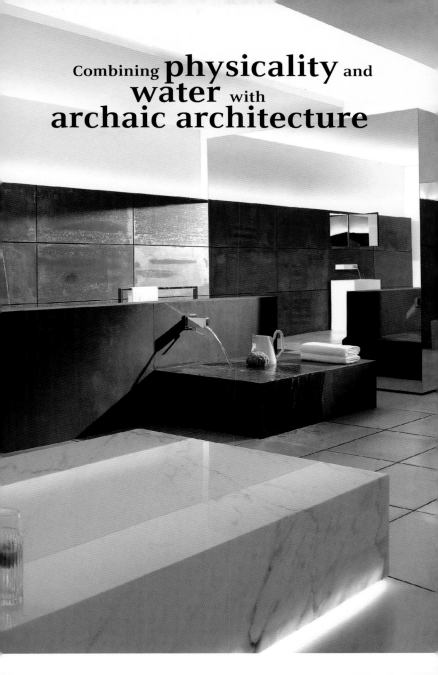

Combining **physicality** and **water** with **archaic architecture**

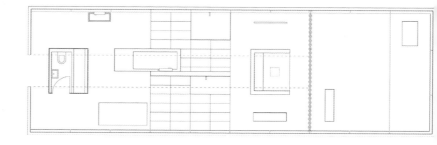

The **only elements** employed here are **water, stone** and **light**

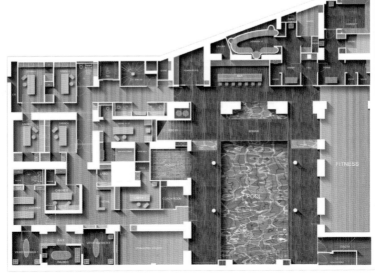

Geleen Bath | Amsterdam | Otello Gatto

Corton rust-finish tiles
combined with **mosaic**

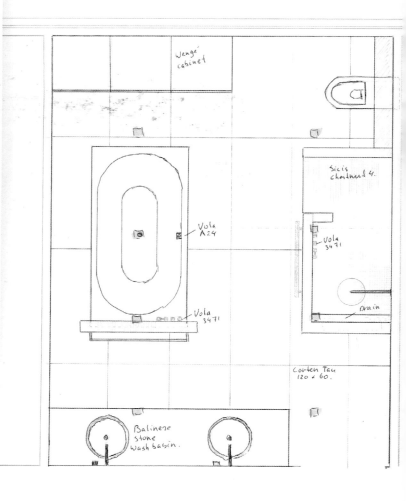

Wengé cabinet

Vola A24

Sicis chestnut 4.

Vola 3471

Vola 3471

Drain

Corten Tau 120 × 60.

Balinese stone wash basin.

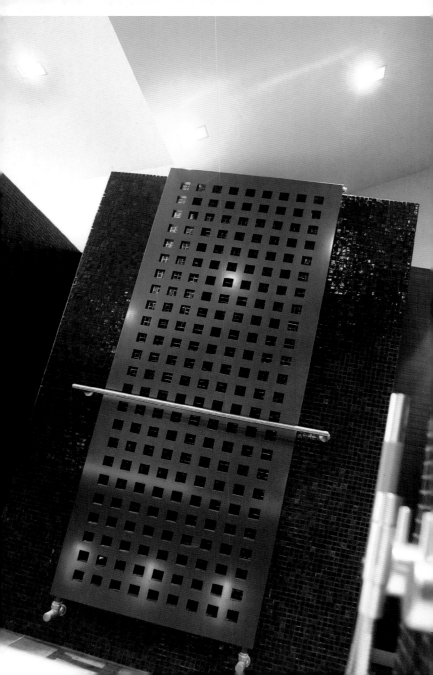

98 | **Hamam Trafo** | Baden | integrales Planungsteam ushitamborriello, Innenarchiotektur & Szenenbild

This **Turkish spa** creates an ambience of **earthy mysticism** with surfaces in different **shades of gray** and **green** and green-lit pools

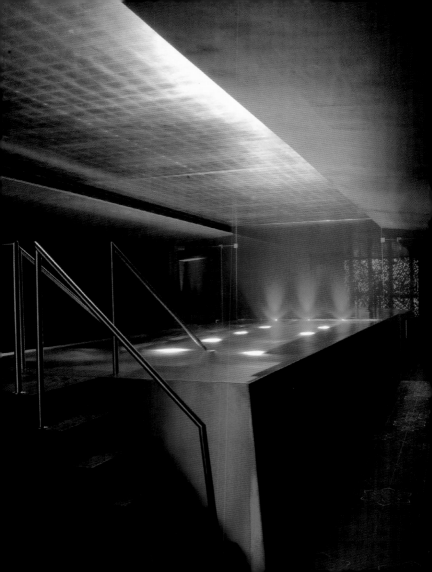

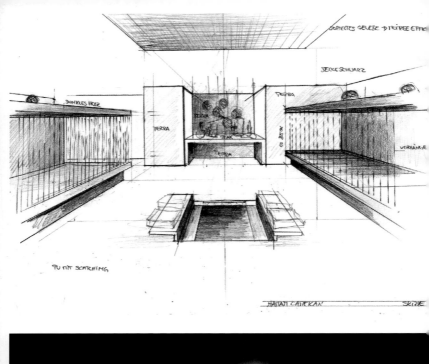

DUNKLES HOLZ

TERRA

TERRA

TEAK

TERRA

TERRA

GELBES GLAS

VORHÄNGE

OBERFLÄCHE GELBE D'ICUREE EFFIC

DECKE SCHWARZ

PU MIT SCRATCHING

HAMAN CATTEKAN   SKIZZE

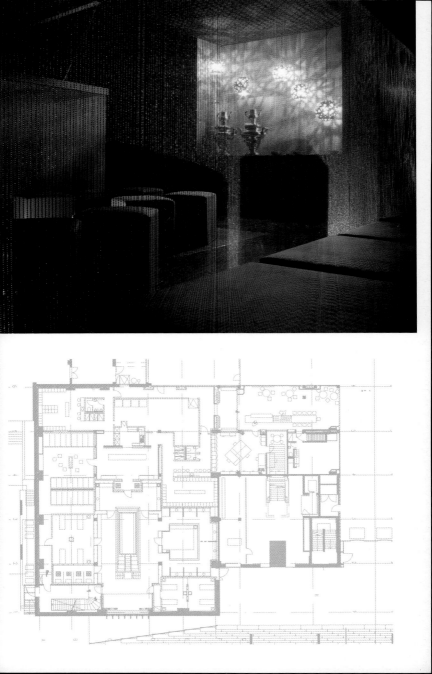

108108 | **Health Center Lanserhof** | Lans near Innsbruck | D E SIGNSTUDIO
Regina Dahmen-Ingenhoven

Soft colors, shapes and materials, **inviting** visitors to **relax** and **regain** their strength

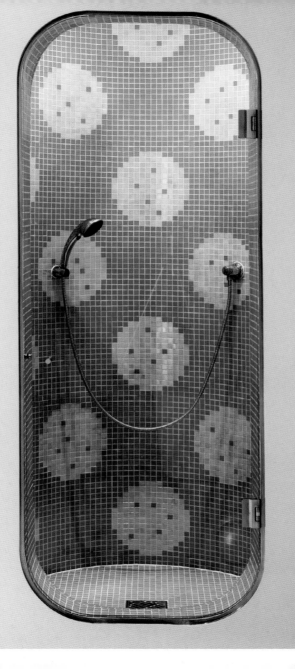

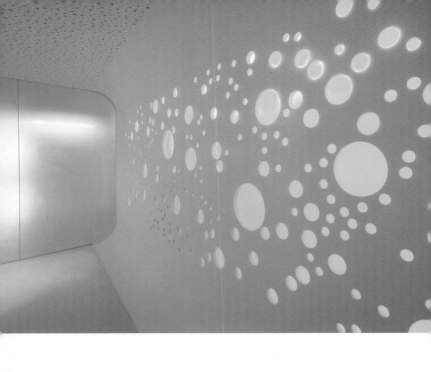

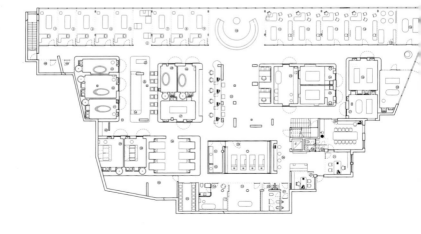

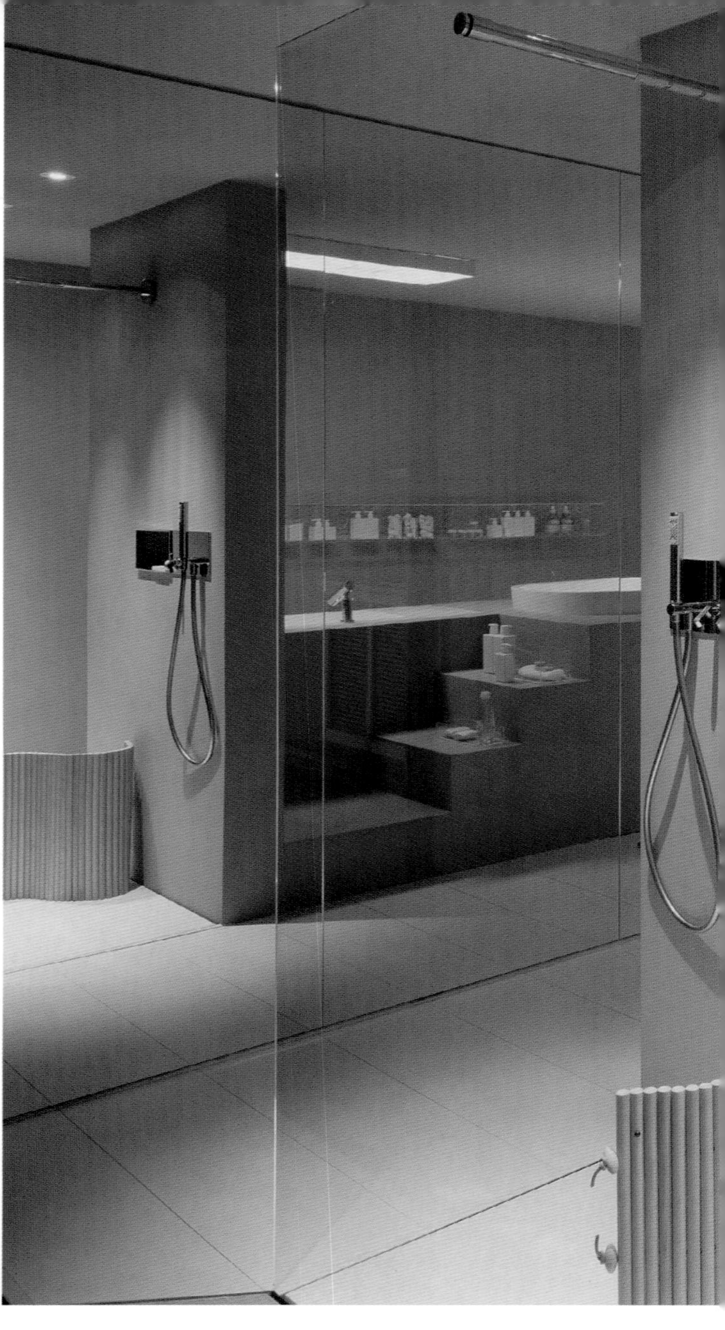

A sequence of
seven settings

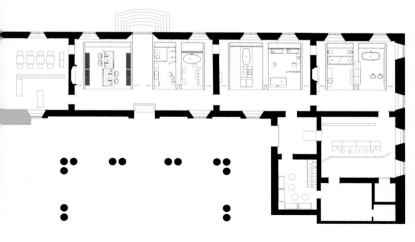

The **light changes** from bright **yellow-orange** in the morning to **dark blue** at night

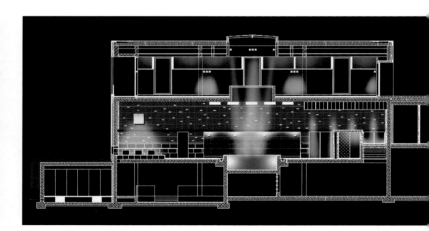

This **hybrid bath-** and **bedroom** allows for **double** functional **occupancy**

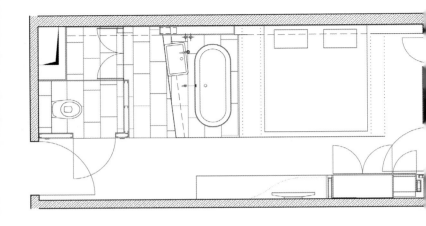

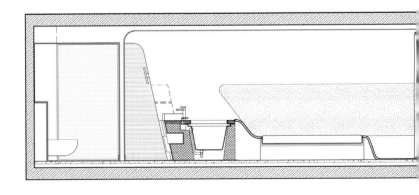

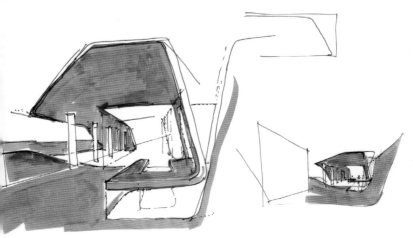

146 | **Kaufman Loft Bath** | New York | Studio Rinaldi

White Thasos **marble mosaic tiles** are combined with **terrazzo floor tiles**

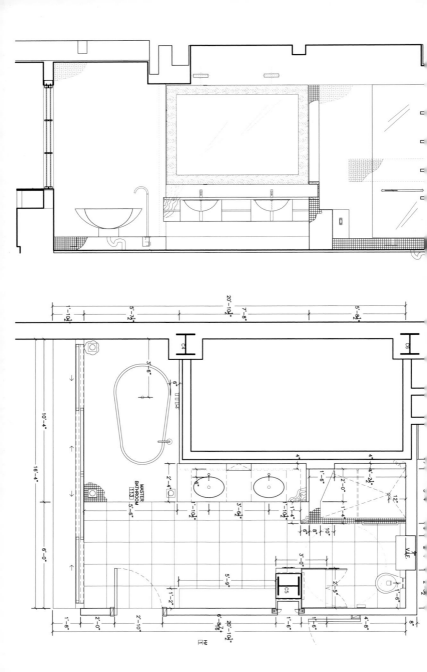

152 | **Kinuta Stone Spa** | Tokyo | Megumi Matsubara & Hiroi Ariyama

This **space creates** a clean and uncluttered **environment** that **draws** its users **into** deep relaxation

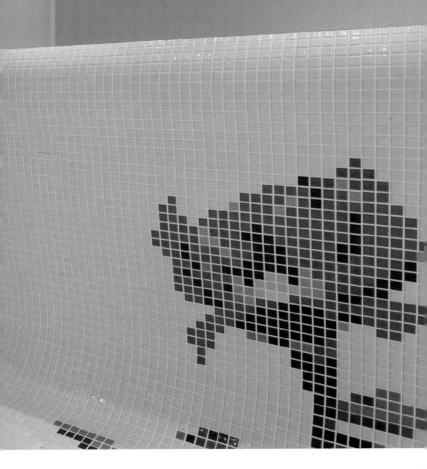

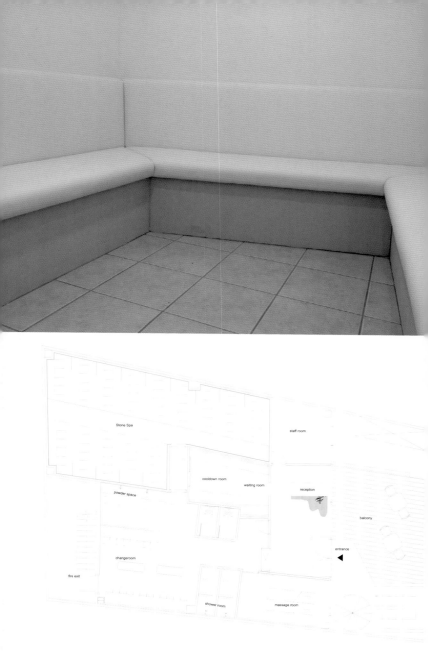

158 | **Kusaba Apartment** | Oita | Takao Shiotsuka Atelier

Concrete and glass walls create a solid yet open space

La Réserve Genève Hotel & Spa | Bellevue | Jacques Garcia

Here is a **rich, luxurious** and **sophisticated** jungle **design** scheme

174 | **Labo Day Spa** | Zurich | Aroma Productions AG

Delicate **composition**
of **natural** materials
and **fine** colors

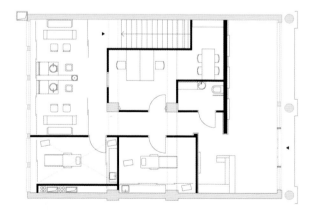

180 | **Liquidrom** | Berlin | gmp – Architekten von Gerkan, Marg und Partner

Light and sound
define the **atmosphere**
of this **space**

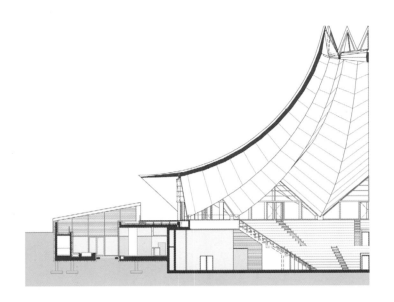

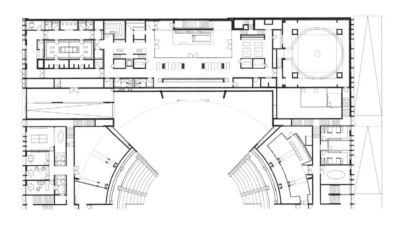

Both **bath** and **shower** **facilities** incorporate the **bright-blue floor**

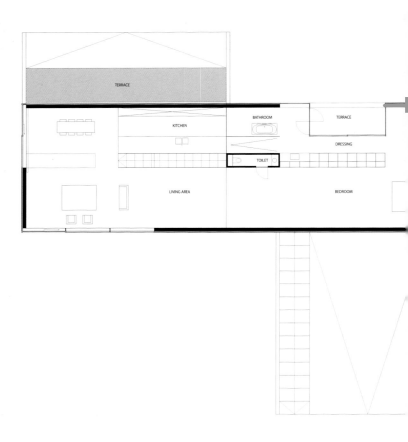

TERRACE

KITCHEN

BATHROOM

TERRACE

DRESSING

TOILET

LIVING AREA

BEDROOM

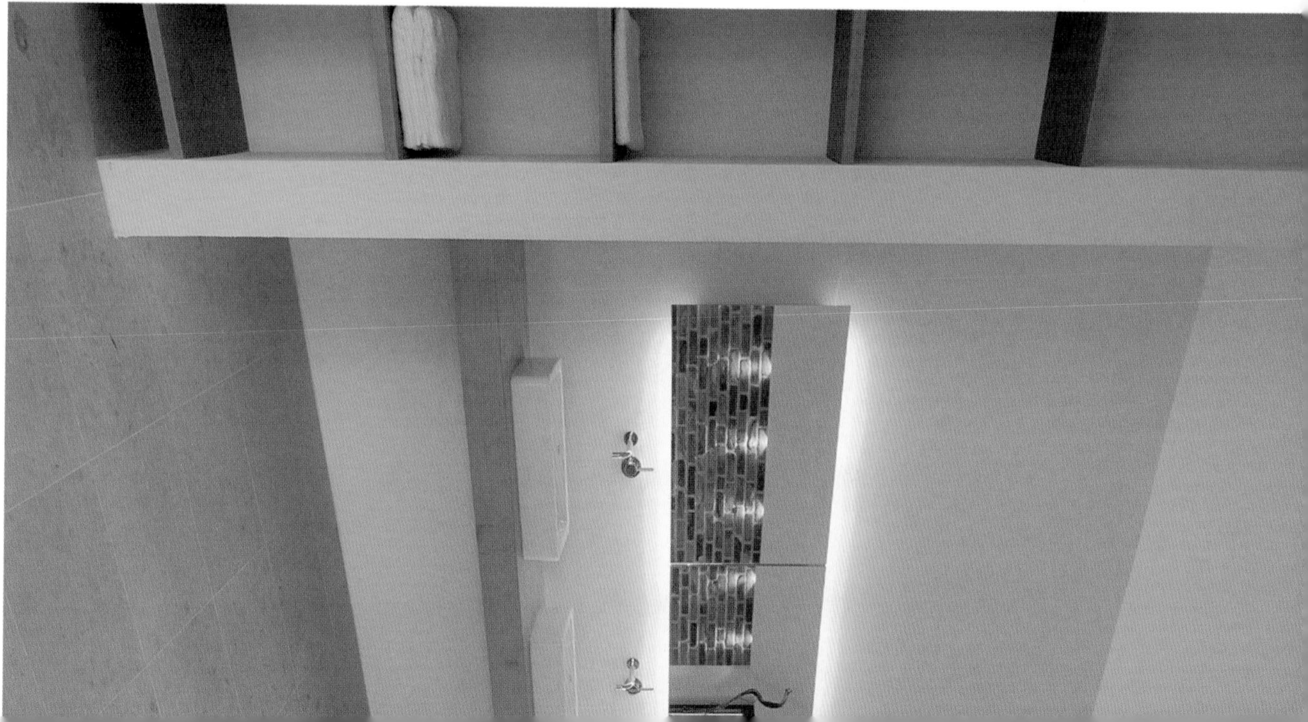

Loft Bathroom | Fulda | BUB architekten

A **spacious shower**
and **isolated tub**
combined with **compact** materials

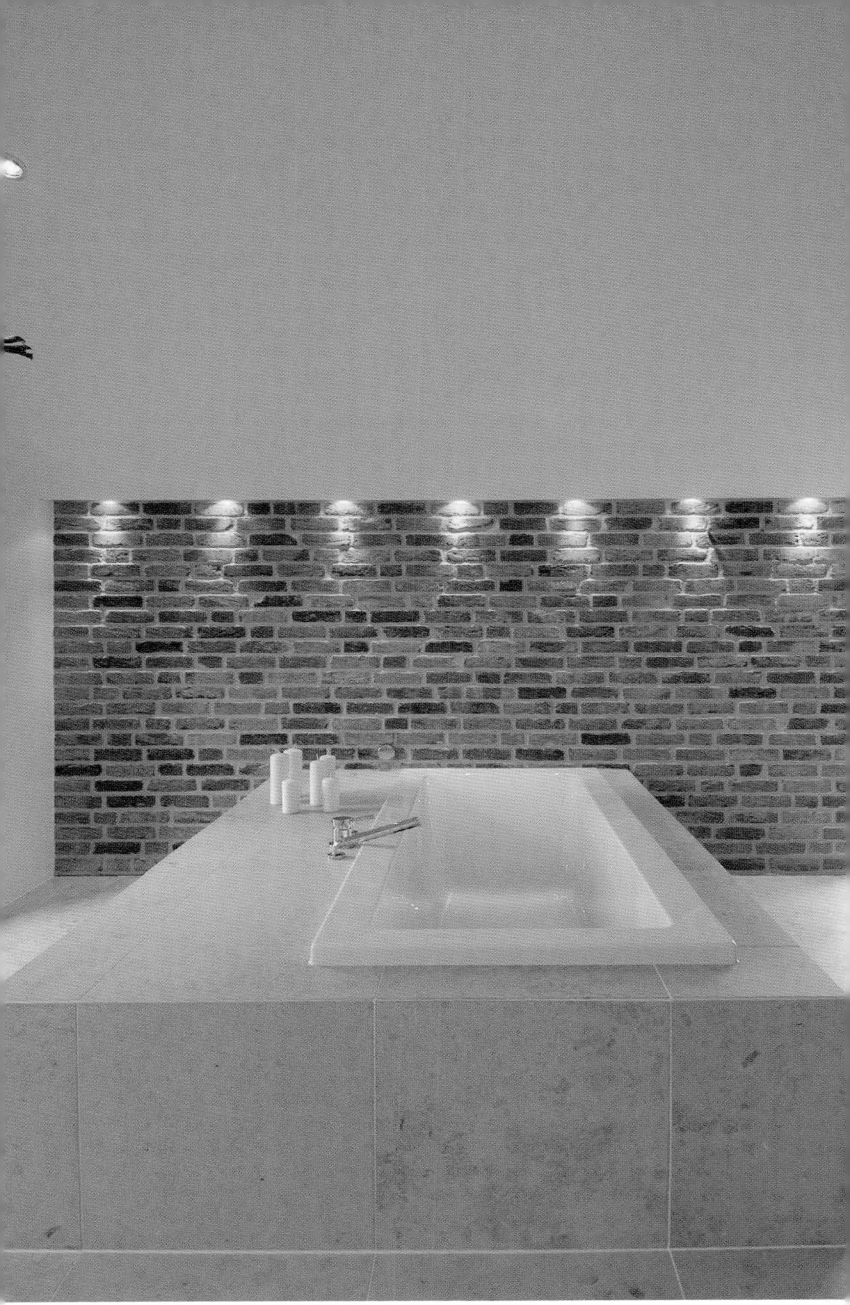

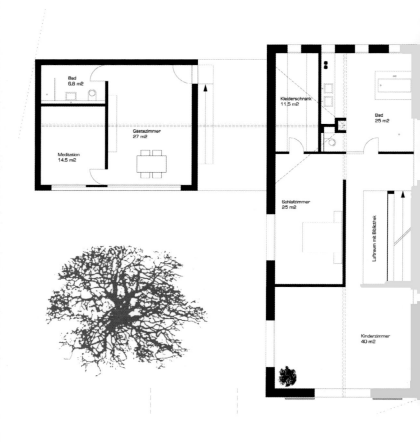

Bad
6.8 m2

Meditation
14.5 m2

Gästezimmer
27 m2

Kleiderschrank
11,5 m2

Bad
25 m2

Schlafzimmer
25 m2

Luftraum mit Bibliothek

Kinderzimmer
40 m2

This design uses zinc fittings, colorful teak motifs and Bisazza mosaic

222 | **McCarthy Residence** | Sydney | stephen varady architecture

Exploring the potential of glass as a modern construction material

Designed to **manifest** the
Swedish ritual
of **sauna** baths

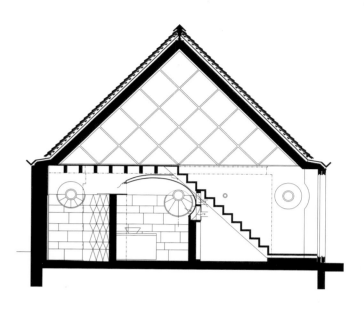

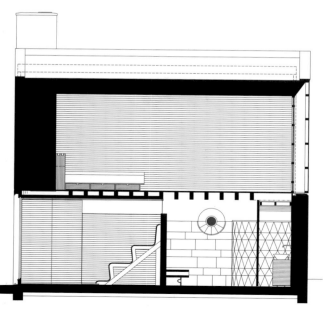

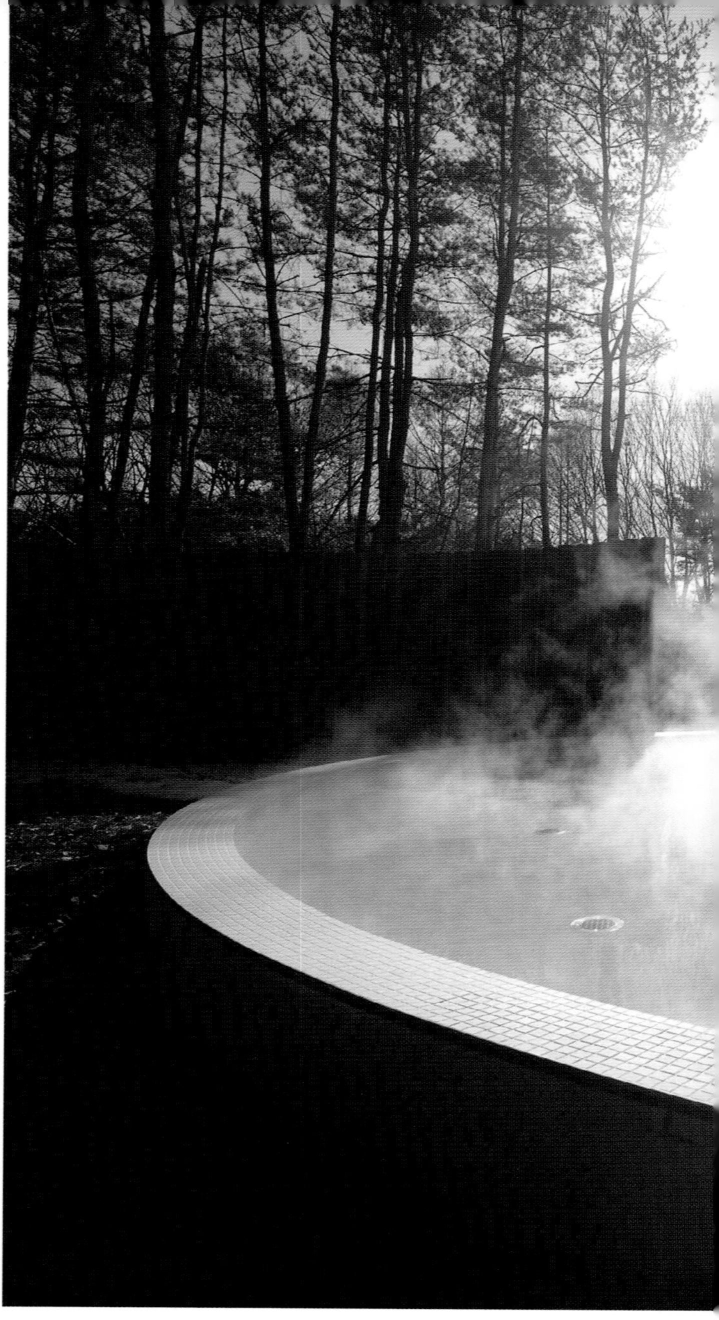

This spa offers **year-round** **bathing** in a **sylvan setting**

246 | **Penthouse Private Bathing Area** | Hamburg | kramer biwer mau architekten

A **bathroom** that **acts** as an **open relaxation zone** between living and **sleeping area**

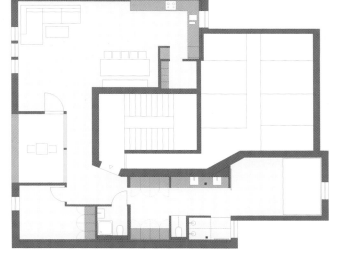

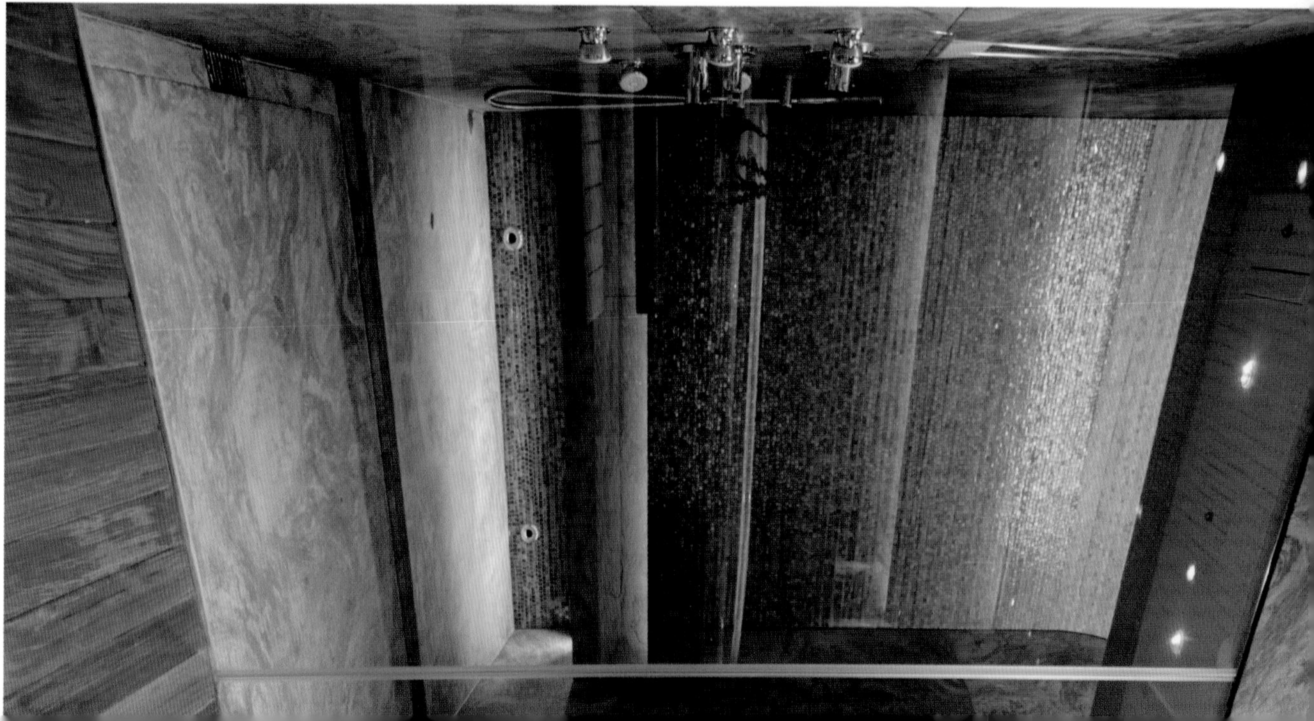

The **harmonious design** offers an excellent **indoor environment** coupled with **superb functionality**

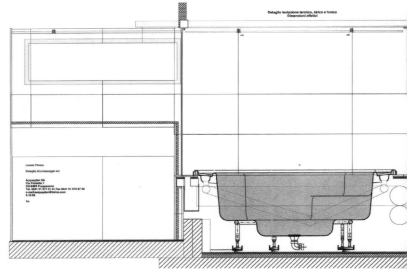

Detaglio isolazione termico, idrico e fonico
Dimensioni effettivi

Locale Fitness

Detaglio chromessaggio est

Acquaplan SA
Via Pedretta 1
CH-6963 Pregassona
Tel. 0041 91 971 21 21 Fax 0041 91 972 87 53
e-mail:acquaplan@ticiino.com
8.10.05

Ao

A very **small bathroom** with a **spacious feeling**

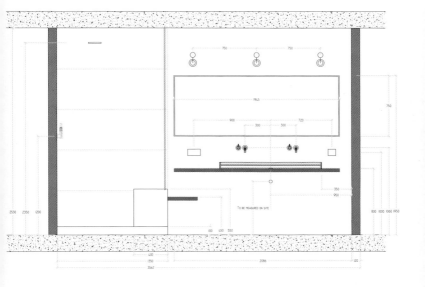

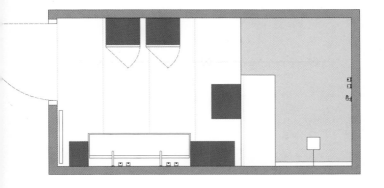

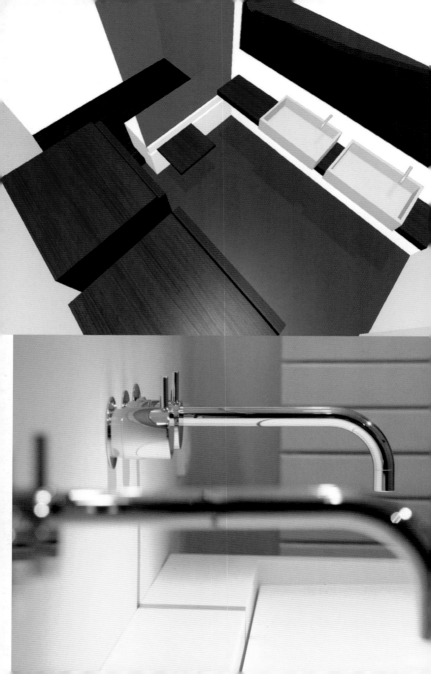

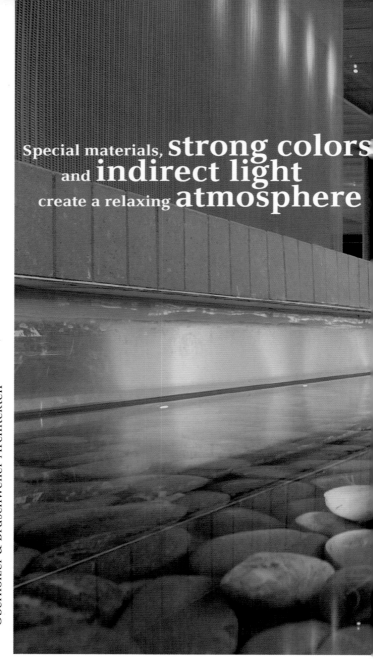

Special materials, **strong colors**
and indirect light
create a relaxing **atmosphere**

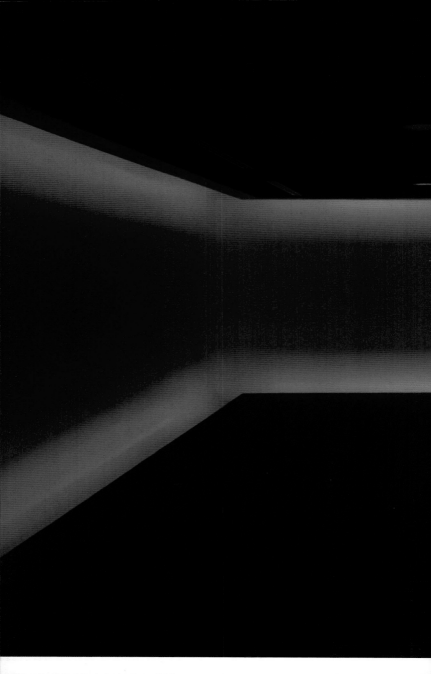

Refurbishment of a Bathroom | Cologne | SEITEN_ANSICHT

Detailed style with
marble cladding

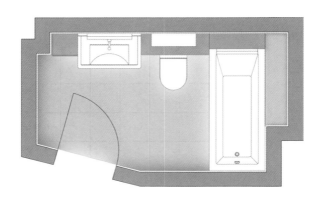

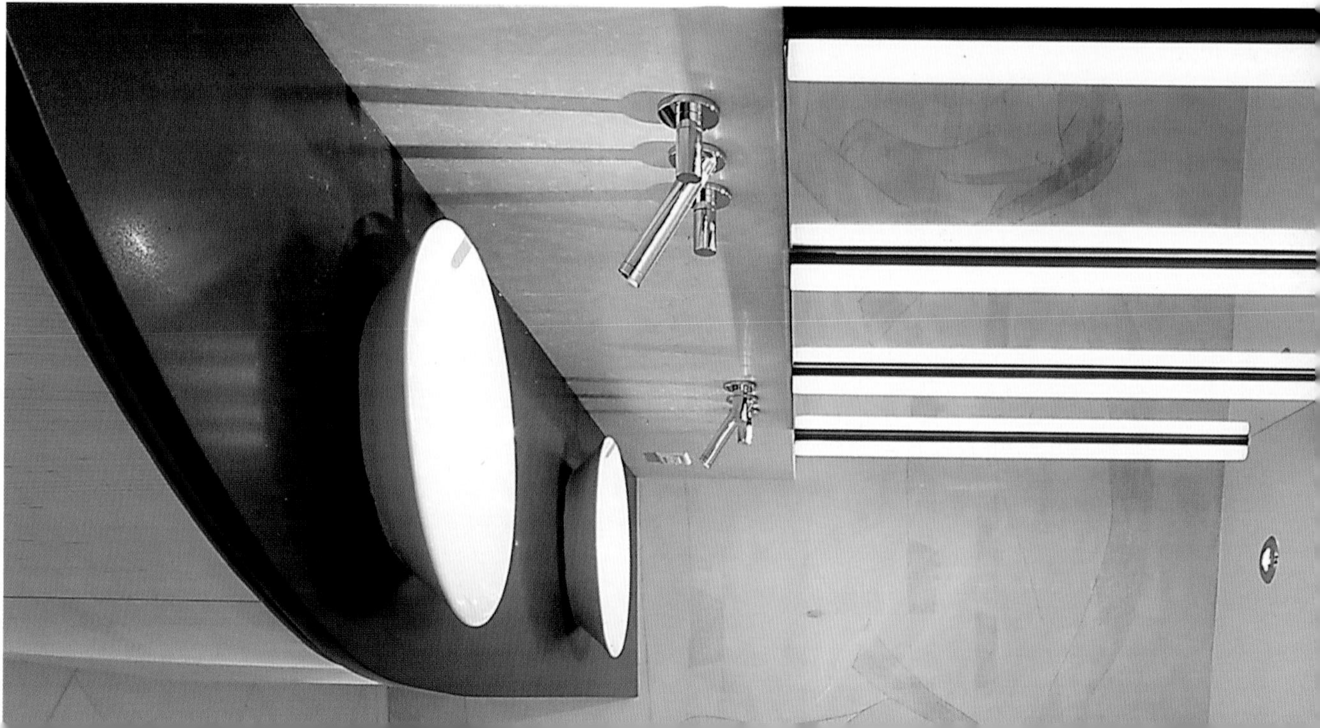

Painted canvases provide depth and artistic allure

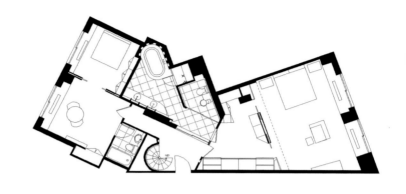

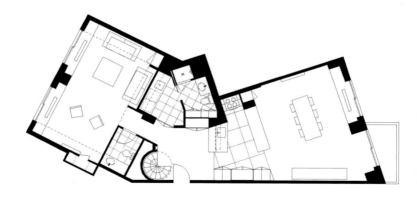

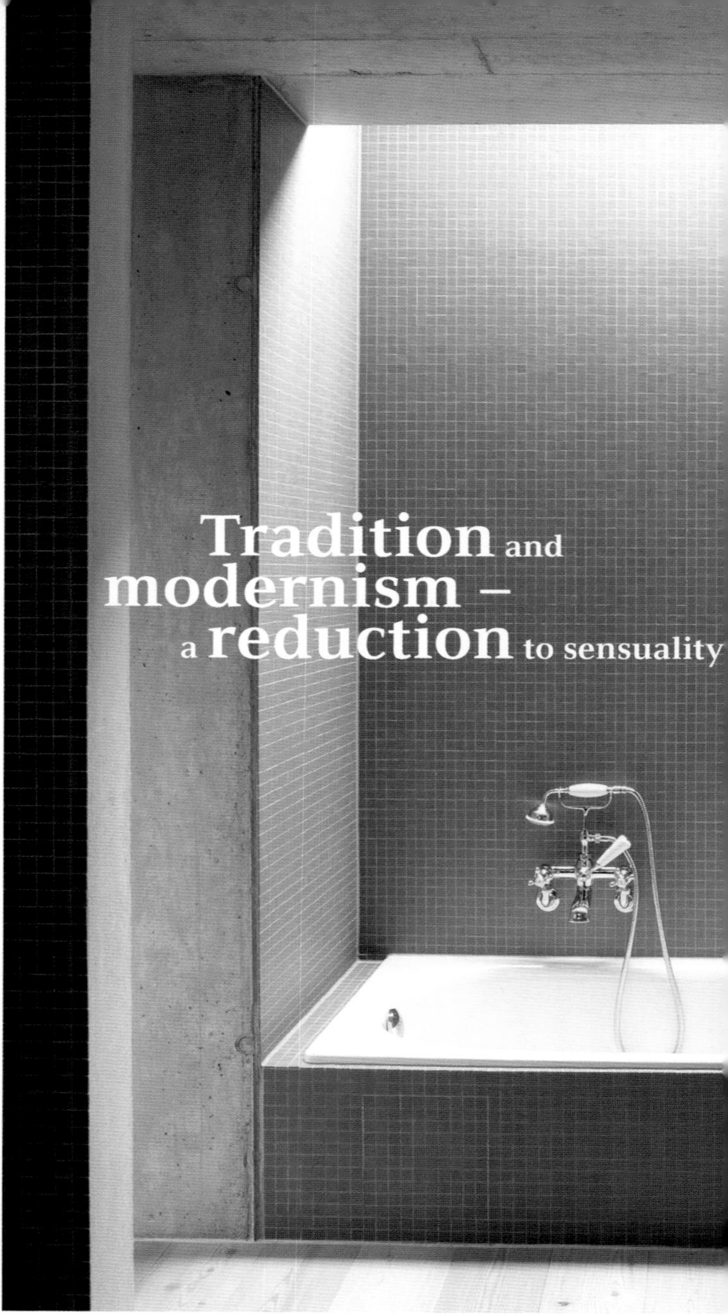

Tradition and
modernism –
a **reduction** to sensuality

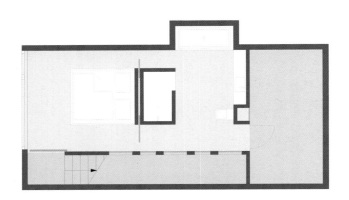

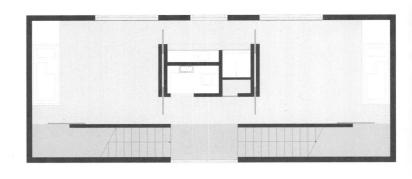

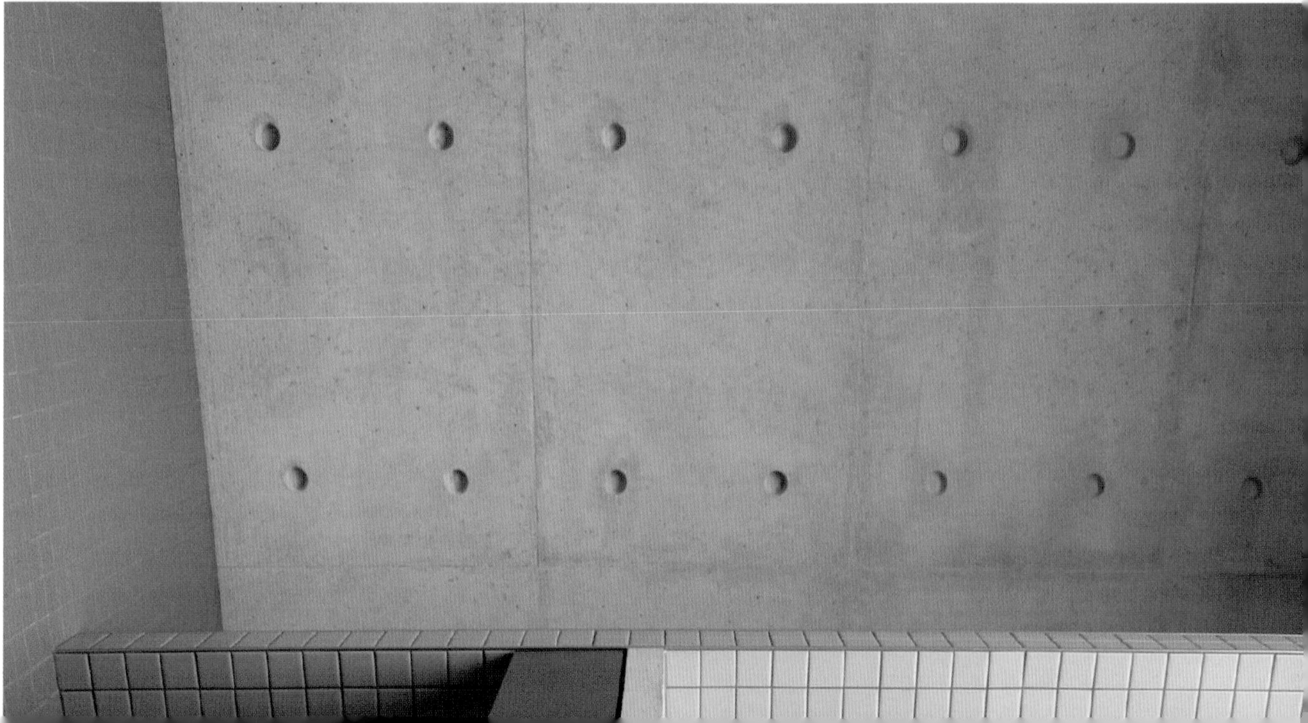

The **concrete structure**
creates a **sublime mood**

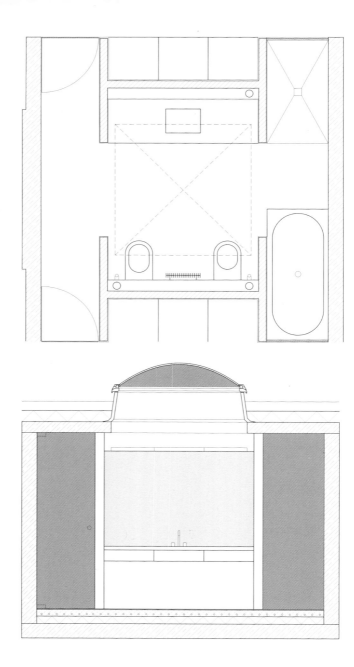

Inviting nature
into the home

Rubin Residence | Bloomfield Hills | McIntosh Poris Associates

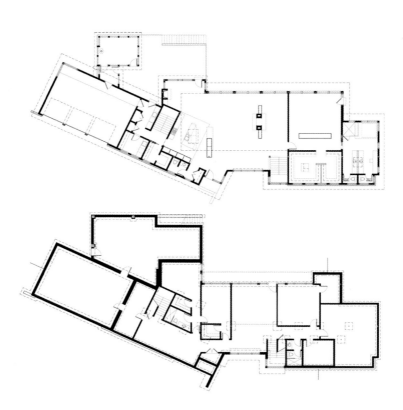

32 | **Silver Rain a La Prairie Spa** | Grand Cayman | Carl D'Aquino & Francine Monaco of D'Aquino Monaco

The guests are **surrounded** by the **comforting aura** of **water** in all its **states**

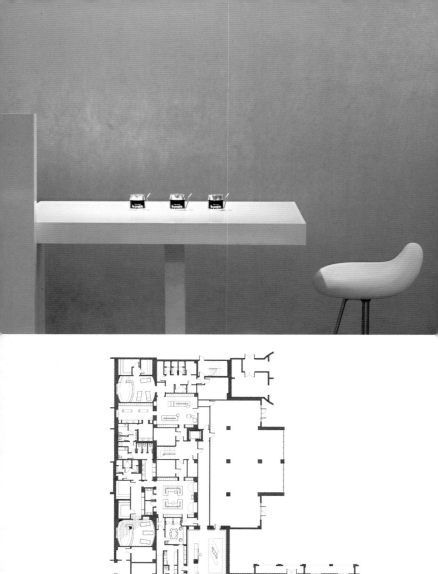

Spa Barn | Nakenstorf near Neukloster | Nalbach + Nalbach | Hon. Prof. Johanne Nalbach

The **bath area** plays with the elements **fire, water and earth**

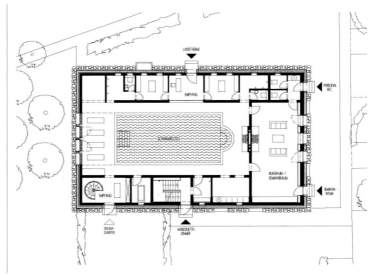

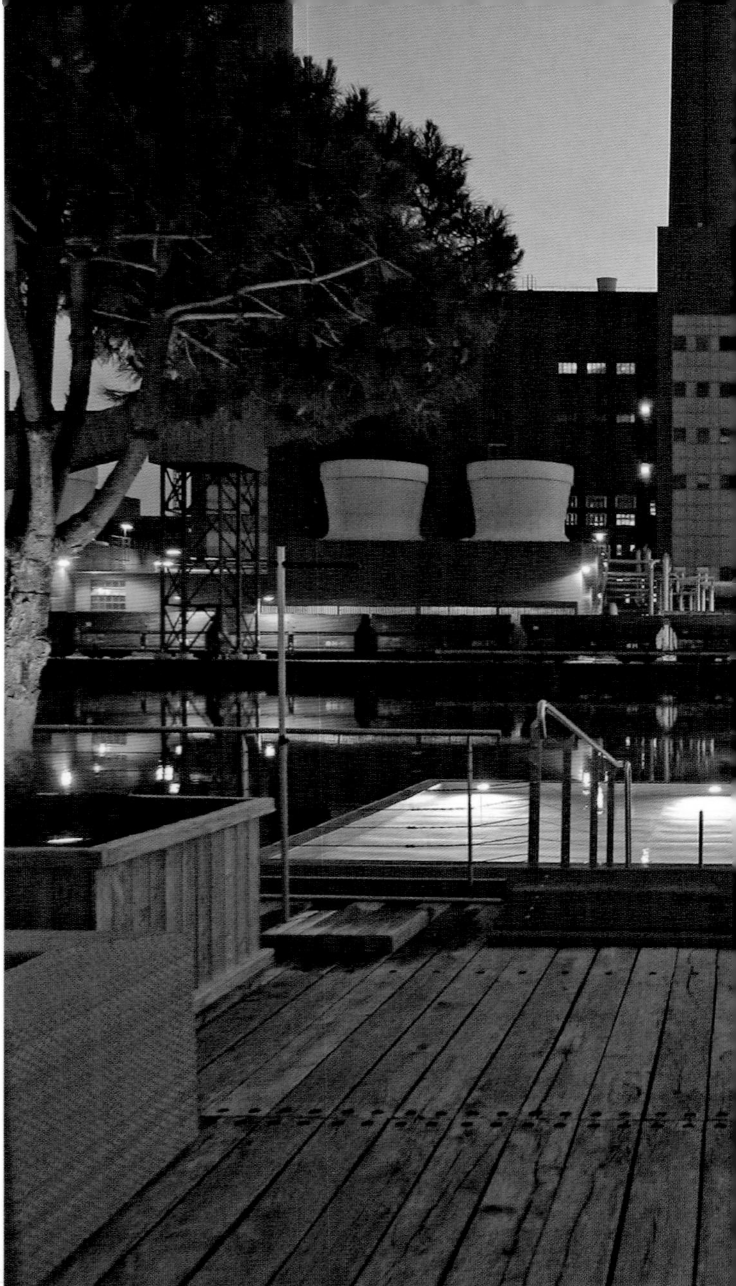

This **spa** consciously employs a
minimalist style
and **pure elements**

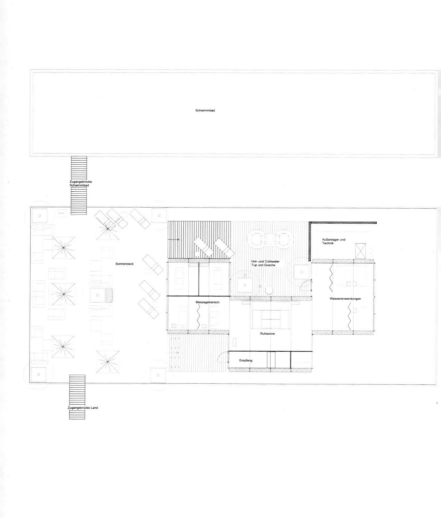

Schwimmbad

Zugangsbrücke
Schwimmbad

Sonnendeck

Hot- und Coldwater
Tup und Dusche

Außenlager und
Technik

Massagebereich

Wasseranwendungen

Ruhezone

Empfang

Zugangsbrücke Land

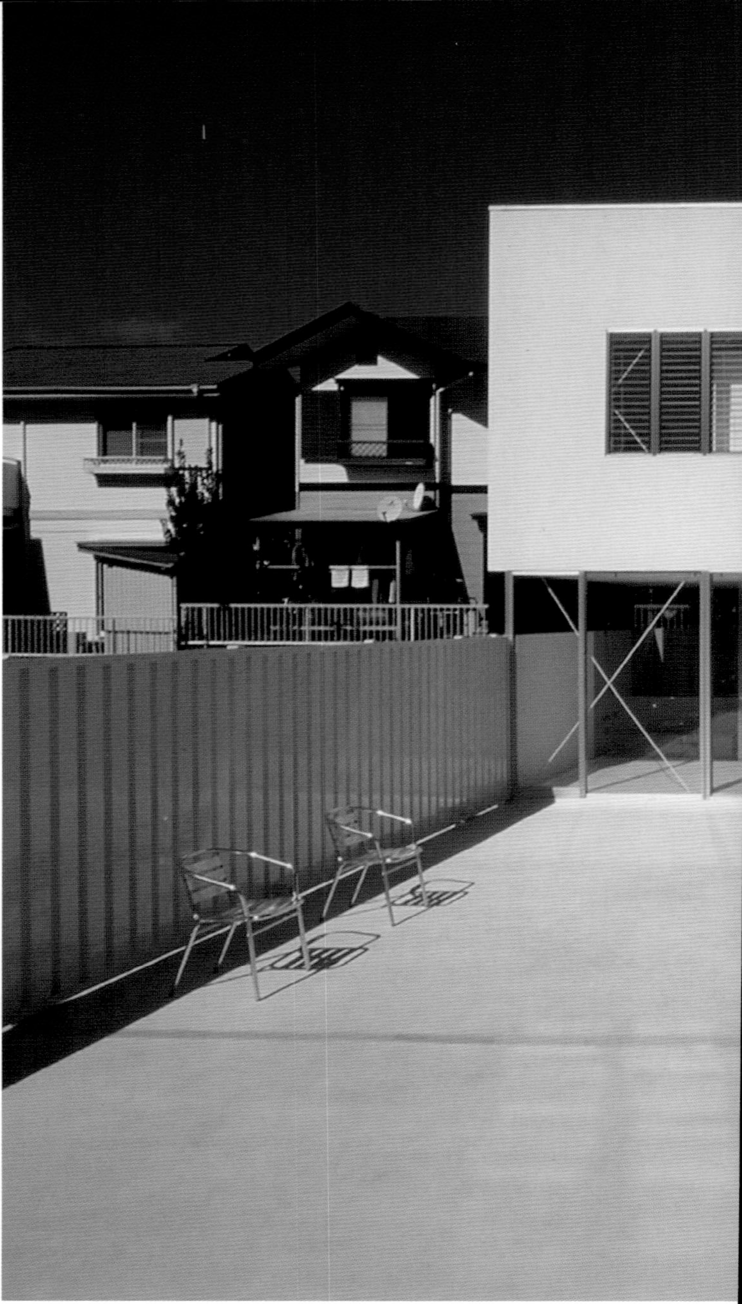

This is a **modern take** on **Japanese Zen design**

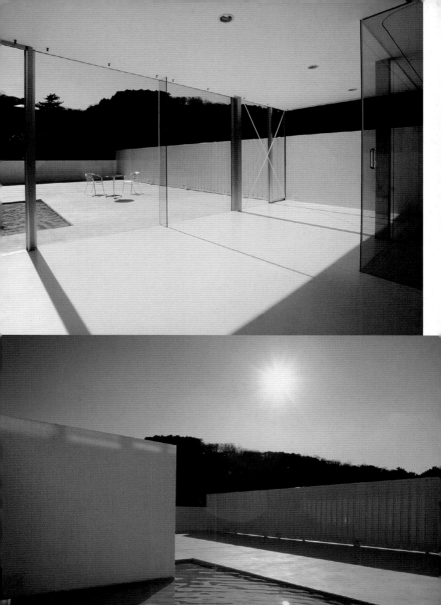

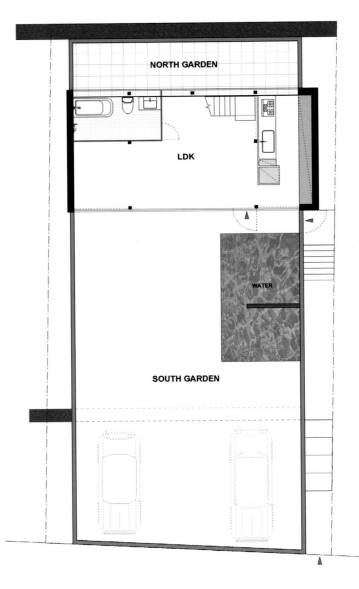

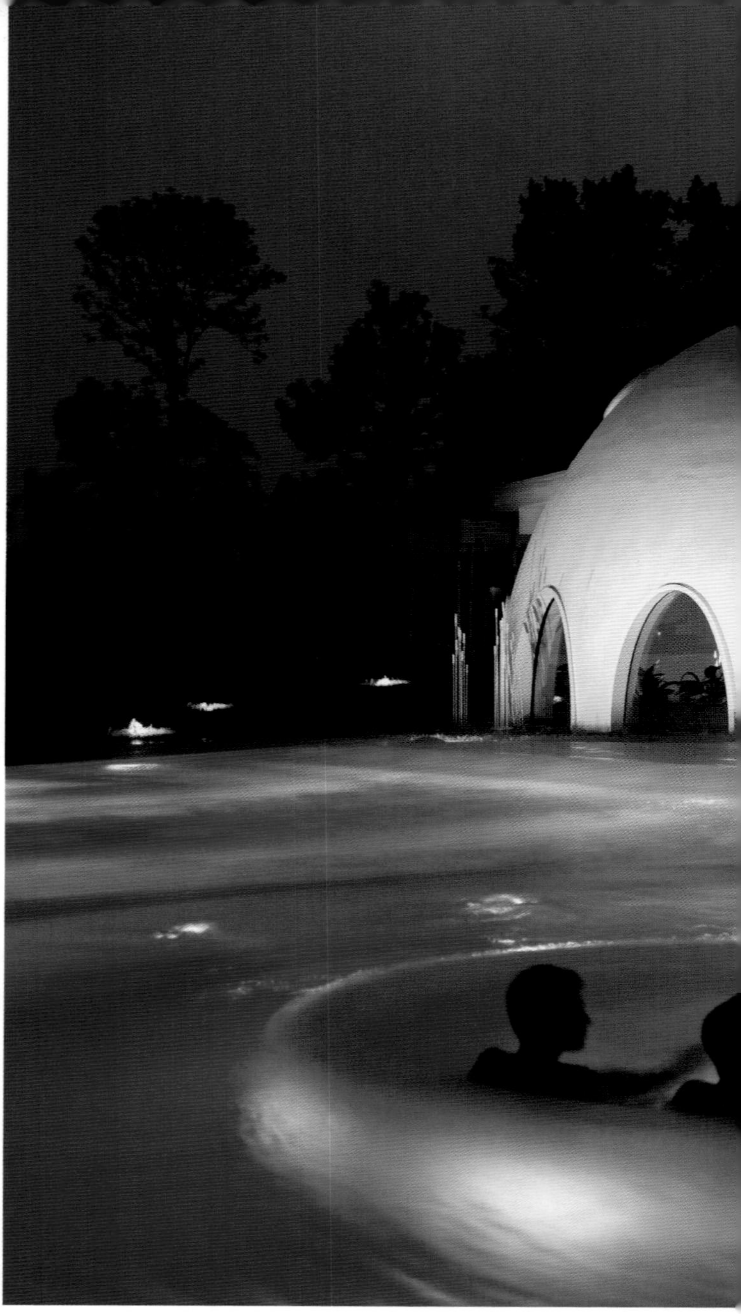

This spa offers **spacious relaxation** areas and a **choice of pools,** baths and **Jacuzzis**

368 | **Tschuggen Bergoase** | Arosa | Mario Botta

A **natural basin** surrounded
by **mountains**

1.40 m

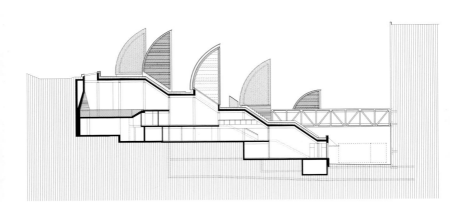

The story-high **green lamellae** create an **introverted ambience**

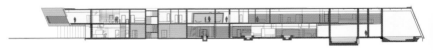

caldarium
50°C

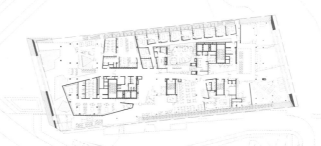

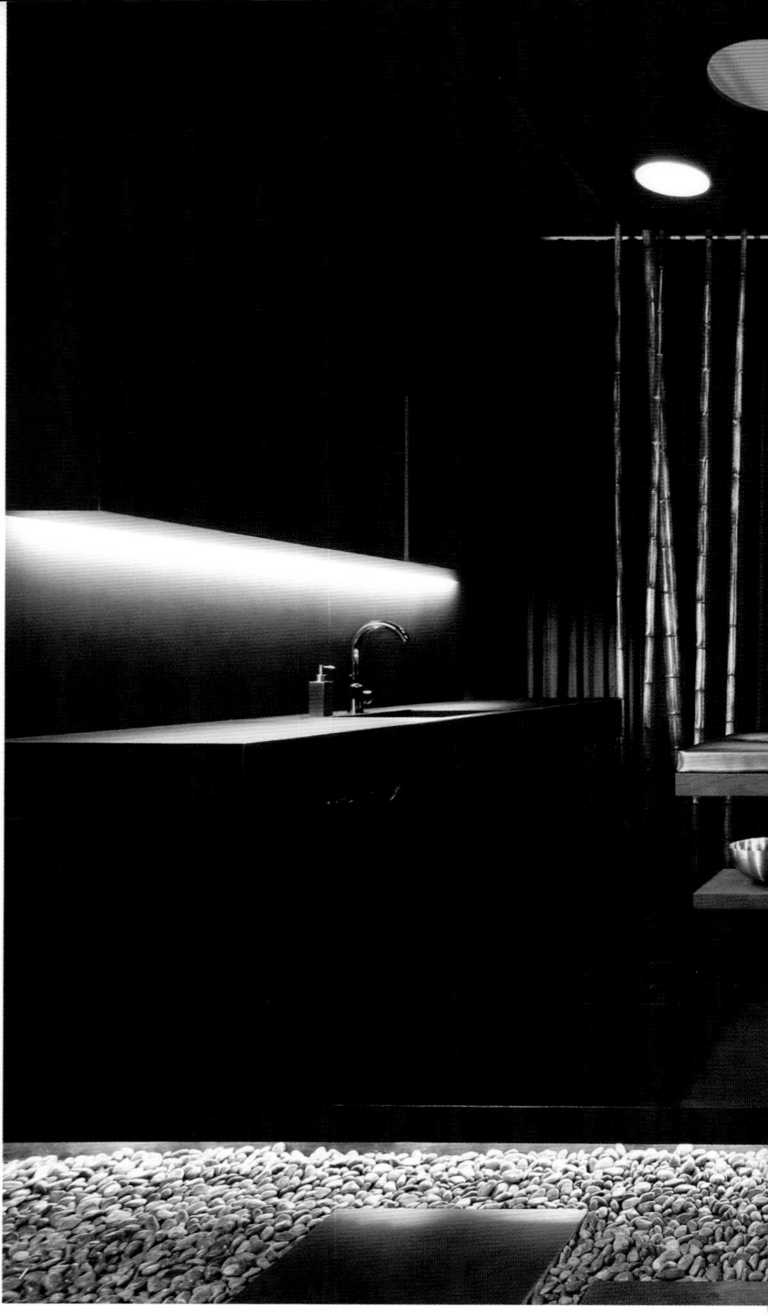

Presenting **holistic lifestyle design** with understated **elegance**

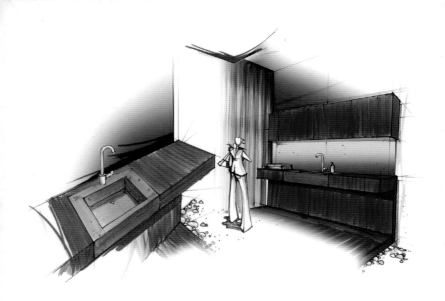

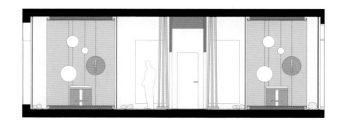

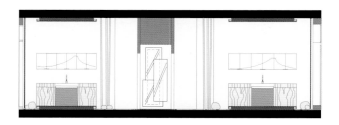

Architects Index

4a Architekten
www.architektenbuero4a.de ► 380

**Carl D'Aquino & Francine Monaco
of D'Aquino Monaco**
www.daquinomonaco.com ► 328

Aroma Productions AG
www.aroma.ch ► 174

Acquaplan
www.acquaplan.ch ► 252

Behnisch Architekten
www.behnisch.com ► 354

**D E SIGNSTUDIO
Regina Dahmen-Ingenhoven**
www.drdi.de ► 108

Giampaolo Benedini Architects
www.benediniassociati.com ► 120

Joseph Caspari
josephcaspari.com ► 78

Crepain Binst Architecture
www.crepainbinst.com ► 190

Mario Botta
www.botta.ch ► 368

**Dirkjan Broekhuizen
Interieurarchitect BNI**
www.dirkjanbroekhuizen.com ► 34

BUB architekten
www.bub-architekten.de ► 200

Büro Wehberg
www.buero-wehberg.de ► 336

Jacques Garcia
www.lareserve.ch ► 166

Otello Gatto
www.gatto.nl ► 88

**gmp – Architekten von
Gerkan, Marg und Partner**
www.gmp-architekten.de ► 180

**Graft – Gesellschaft von
Architekten mbH**
www.graftlab.com ► 138

Grassl Haertwig Architekten
www.grassl-haertwig.de ► 130

Hennings Börn Interiors
www.hennings-börn.de ► 10

Klein Dytham architecture
www.klein-dytham.com ► 236

kramer biwer mau architekten
www.kbm-architelten.de ► 246

G. Hakan Kulahci
www.artmim.com.tr ► 58

lohrmannarchitekt
www.lohrmannarchitekt.de ► 294

Loodszeven Interieurarchitecten
www.loodszeven.nl ► 262

Megumi Matsubara &
Hiroi Ariyama
www.withassistant.net ► 152

McIntosh Poris Associates
www.mcintoshporis.com
► 314

Meiré und Meiré
www.meireundmeire.de ► 68

monovolume
www.monovolume.cc ► 16

Nalbach + Nalbach
Hon. Prof. Johanne Nalbach
www.nalbach-architekten.de ► 328

N Maeda Atelier
www5a.biglobe.ne.jp ► 346

Axel Nieberg
www.nieberg-architect.de ► 306

Oberholzer & Brüschweiler
Architekten
www.wodb-arch.ch ► 270

plajer & franz studio
www.plajer-franz.de ► 388

PrastHooft
www.prasthooft.nl ► 42

Leopoldo Rosati Architecture
www.leopoldorosati.com ► 286

Richardson Sadeki
www.richardsonsadeki.com ► 22

SEITEN_ANSICHT
www.seiten-ansicht.de ► 280

integrales Planungsteam
Ushi Tamborriello, Innenarchitek-
tur & Szenenbild
www.tamborriello.de ► 98, 270

Takao Shiotsuka Atelier
www.shio-atl.com ► 158

Studio Rinaldi
www.studiosrinaldi.com ► 146

stephen varady architecture
www.stephenvarady.com ► 222

Venlet Interior Architecture bvba
www.venlet.net ► 50

Marcel Wanders Studio
www.marcelwanders.nl ► 210

Wingårdh
www.wingardhs.se ► 226